Springer Series on Cultural Computing

Cultural Computing is an exciting, emerging field of Human Computer Interaction, which covers the cultural impact of computing and the technological influences and requirements for the support of cultural innovation. Using support technologies such as artificial intelligence, machine learning, location-based systems, mixed/virtual/augmented reality, cloud computing, pervasive technologies and human-data interaction, researchers can explore the differences across a variety of cultures and cultural production to provide the knowledge and skills necessary to overcome cultural issues and expand human creativity.

This series presents monographs, edited collections and advanced textbooks on the current research and knowledge of a broad range of topics including creativity support systems, creative computing, digital communities, the interactive arts, cultural heritage, digital culture and intercultural collaboration.

This Series is abstracted/indexed in Scopus.

Francesca Franco
Editor

Computational Art at the Venice Biennale (1970–2015)

Springer

Editor
Francesca Franco
College of Humanities
University of Exeter
Exeter, Devon, UK

ISSN 2195-9056 ISSN 2195-9064 (electronic)
Springer Series on Cultural Computing
ISBN 978-3-032-04257-6 ISBN 978-3-032-04258-3 (eBook)
https://doi.org/10.1007/978-3-032-04258-3

This Springer imprint is published by the registered company Springer Nature Switzerland AG
The registered company address is: Gewerbestrasse 11, 6330 Cham, Switzerland

Acknowledgments

This book is based on research and interviews conducted over the past 15 years with artists and critics who have directly experienced and exhibited at the Venice Biennale. I am immensely grateful to the contributors of this volume—Fré Ilgen, Maureen Kendal, Maria Grazia Mattei, Frieder Nake, Joseph Nechvatal, Simon Pope, Tamiko Thiel, and Paul Thomas—for their generosity in sharing their valuable insights on their work and for the many conversations we had that have inspired this publication.

A special word of gratitude is due to the Computer Arts Society, its chair and committee members, who have supported me throughout the years and have been instrumental in making this project a reality. I am particularly grateful to Nick Lambert, Paul Brown, Ernest Edmonds, and Sean Clark for their constant encouragement and support. I would also like to thank Orly Aviv who kindly granted permission to publish her images.

Finally, I would like to express my heartfelt thanks to my editor, Helen Desmond, who has followed this journey with enormous patience, thoughtful guidance, and unwavering support. Her editorial insight and careful choices have been invaluable in shaping this book, and I am deeply grateful for her commitment throughout the process. I would also like to thank everyone at Springer for their assistance—especially Jacob Shmulewitz, Editorial Assistant, for his kind and attentive help.

Contents

Introduction

Francesca Franco

Looking for computer art at the Venice Biennale is always a fascinating and exciting adventure. As art critic Adrian Searle observed at the opening of the 2013 event, “The Venice Biennale is always too big, too diffuse, too sprawling and too filled with divergent objects, images and ideas to make any coherent sense” (Searle 2013). Looking for computer art there is an even more challenging task, owing to its hybrid, fluid nature, and by the fact that this art, using the computer as a tool or medium, although around from the 1960s, has not been fully accepted by traditional art institutions and has been overlooked for many years.

There are a number of reasons for why the Venice Biennale is worth investigating. Firstly, the Biennale is the oldest international festival of contemporary art in the world and has been fully documented since its very beginning in 1895. It therefore represents an invaluable historical account and source of information for any individual interested in understanding the development of contemporary art from an array of diverse perspectives. More importantly, by documenting such a wide historical period, the Biennale has encompassed and witnessed the introduction of computer art into the art world. Secondly, by being international in scope, the Biennale embodies a range of aesthetic visions that may reflect both the diversities or the common taste of an era in the art historical domain. It is therefore fundamental, and extremely illuminating, when analysing an interdisciplinary subject such as computer art and its multifaceted origins. Thirdly, the intrinsic nature of the Biennale of being a recurring festival, as opposed to the notion of the fixed, “stable” role of the traditional art museum, has allowed the institution to adjust itself to historical and political circumstances, both national and international. Owing to the Biennale’s ever-changing nature, its curatorial projects have offered the audience a miniature reflection of the broader changes that have happened in the world at large.

F. Franco (✉)
College of Humanities, University of Exeter, Exeter, UK

F. Franco (ed.), *Computational Art at the Venice Biennale (1970–2015)*, Springer Series on Cultural Computing, https://doi.org/10.1007/978-3-032-04258-3_1

Historically, the first Biennales, particularly between 1895 and 1914, were devoted to the celebration of the official academic style, or "Salon art" (Alloway 1969). Far from being innovative and open to the new European tendencies, the first Biennales demonstrated a conservative and reassuring attitude towards art.

The initial Venice Biennale's curatorial model changed owing to political circumstances in 1968, the year of European radical revolts for social and economic reform. From a curatorial perspective, the 1968 Biennale represented an "anomaly" compared to its previous renditions. Not only the political instances brought forward by the student revolt but also the introduction of new technologies in art from the mid 1960s contributed and allowed the institution to distance itself from its original nineteenth-century Salon model. Owing to innovative and cross-disciplinary projects such as those presented by Argentinean artist David Lamelas and French cybernetic artist Nicolas Schöffer at the 1968 Biennale, the institution started, slowly, to open up towards new media and to accept them as a new form of art. From then on, the acceptance of media art by the biennale increased in pace. It was particularly the 1970 edition that represented one of the key steps for the art institution in the long journey toward the acceptance of computer art (Franco 2013). The Biennale's major show, *Research and Planning—Proposals for an Experimental Exhibition*, was exhibited at the Giardini and curated by Umbro Apollonio and Dietrich Mahlow. The exhibition was entirely centred on "experimental" art and included a large selection of early computer-generated works arranged thematically. They included what are now considered to be iconic pieces such as *Return to a Square* by the Computer Technique Group (1967); *Quadrate (Squares)* by Herbert W. Franke (1970); *Matrix Multiplication* by Frieder Nake (1968); a series of lithographs on paper from computer-generated graphics by Georg Nees; works by Auro Lecci, using an IBM 7090 machine and a Calcomp 563 plotter; and a computer-generated sculpture by Richard C. Raymond. The 1970 show was a rare cutting-edge exhibition, particularly for the Biennale's standards. It was an "anomaly", not a tradition, and it demonstrated for the first time in Venice that computer art could be seen as a way to find a vital function of art in contemporary art institutions.

The mid 1980s witnessed the first genuine attempt of historicisation of computer art, initiated mainly by the work of American art historian Patric Prince. Her major retrospective of computer art organised at SIGGRAPH in 1986 was key in this respect.[1] This can be seen as an essential factor that helped make computer art "safe" and allowed it to be accepted by conservative art institutions worldwide, particularly the Venice Biennale.

The aperture of the Biennale towards art and technology in the 1980s—anticipated by the 1970s *Research and Planning* show—started timidly in 1980 with a peripheral show, *Cronografie* (Chronographs), curated by Italian historian

[1] The SIGGRAPH 1986 art show was connected to the SIGGRAPH 1986 Conference, Convention Centre, Dallas. Patric Prince, chair of the SIGGRAPH 1986 exhibition, chose that year as a historical turning point to celebrate the 25th anniversary of computer art. To mark this anniversary Prince invited most computer art pioneers to present their works. The exhibition featured a total of 450 works and included 6 h of animations, 2 projected installations, and 18 interactive and online works. Exhibiting artists included Manuel Barbadillo, Paul Brown, Charles Csuri, Billy Culver, Jeremy Gardiner, Kenneth Knowlton, Masao Komura, Ben Laposky, Manfred Mohr, Vera Molnar, and Frieder Nake.

Gianfranco Bettettini in collaboration with art historian Gillo Dorfles, architect Ugo La Pietra, and Cesare Blasi. The show was dedicated to the role of memory and time in contemporary society with a focus on new technologies. The section *Memory and Information Technology* in particular presented the latest experiments in computer graphics and art. The Computer Art Society (CAS) was invited to present a selection of works informed by computer technology there. John Lansdown, co-founder of CAS, organised the society's contribution to the show that included, amongst others, works by Dominic Boreham and Paul Brown (*Modulus (8)* series, 1979).

The openness of the Biennale towards art and technology unfolded more rapidly in the mid 1980s, particularly with its 1986 exhibition around the theme of *Art and Science* directed by art historian Maurizio Calvesi. One of its sections, *Technology and Informatics* at the Arsenal's Corderie, was one of the most cutting-edge projects presented there. It showcased *Networking*, an exhibition curated by Roy Ascott, Don Foresta, Tom Sherman, and Tommaso Trini. A triumph of interactive installations by Waltraut Cooper, Brian Eno, Piero Fogliati, Liliane Lijn, Maurizio Mochetti, David Rokeby, and Bill Viola stood side by side with a "laboratory-workshop" that presented videotext artworks selected by Red Burns; a small section on laser disc creations; a "computer imaging" section including computer-generated artworks by Adriano Abbado, Olivier Agid, Roberto Sebastian Matta, and Anne Marie Pecheur; and a personal contribution by Ascott and Robert Adrian, *Planetary Network*, that explored the notion of telematic interactivity.

In the 1990s, art and technology—particularly video art—became openly accepted, exhibited, and eventually awarded. In 1990, for instance, American artist Jenny Holzer received the Biennale's Best Pavilion Award, and in 1993, Korean-born American video artist Nam June Paik was awarded the same prestigious award for his video installation *The Sistine Chapel*. In 1999, Doug Aitken won the Golden Lion for his *Electric Earth* video installation.

Except for the rare case represented by the 1970 Biennale's *Research and Planning* show, computer art at the Biennale has since been exhibited predominantly outside the official site of the Giardini.

This publication brings together a collection of chapters written by five artists—Simon Pope, Tamiko Thiel, Joseph Nechvatal, Fré Ilgen, and Frieder Nake—whose work has been engaged in the various manifestations of art and technology and who have featured at, or made an intervention in, the Venice Biennale over the past 50 years. Their contributions offer a unique perspective on how art and technology have been presented at the Biennale first-hand and how Venice and the Biennale have influenced or inspired the participating artists and their work. The book also includes Maureen Kendal's review of *Nervous Organ*, a digital interactive installation by media artist Orly Aviv exhibited at the 2015 Biennale, providing a comprehensive exploration of contemporary digital art showcased at the event. Furthermore, the author's article on the impact of new media art on the Venice Biennale's original curatorial model post-1968 adds a historical dimension to the examination of the evolving relationship between technology and this prestigious art institution.

In his chapter, Simon Pope discusses his experience representing Wales at the 2003 Biennale and how the work he presented there has evolved from its initial concept up to the present time. In *Site Venice Site Biennale: The Manifest.AR Augmented Reality Intervention into the 2011 Venice Biennale*, Tamiko Thiel provides insight into the international artist collective Manifest.AR and their intervention using geolocative augmented reality during the 2011 Biennale. In *vOluptuary drOid dé-cOlletage at the 55th International Art Exhibition of la Biennale di Venezia*, Joseph Nechvatal situates his work within *Noise*, a collateral event of the 2013 Biennale based on his notion of the "art of noise". Fré Ilgen's contribution describes his experience as a participating artist in the collateral event *Frontiers Reimagined*, held at Palazzo Grimani during the 2015 Biennale. The book includes Maureen Kendal's review of *Nervous Organ*, a digital interactive installation by media artist Orly Aviv exhibited at the 2015 Biennale, and an interview between Francesca Franco and computer art pioneer Frieder Nake, in which Nake reflects on his participation in the first computer art show organised at the Biennale in 1970.

Additionally, two in-depth interviews enrich the volume with curatorial and theoretical insights. In conversation with Francesca Franco, Paul Thomas revisits the landmark 1986 Venice Biennale and reflects on issues of artistic integrity, institutional constraints, and the precarious preservation of digital art. His perspective—rooted in both theory and practice—underscores the need for more organic, artist-led approaches to documenting and understanding media art's cultural legacy. In a complementary interview, Maria Grazia Mattei shares her trajectory as a journalist, critic, and "digital evangelist", tracing the evolution of Italy's engagement with digital culture from the 1980s to today. She offers a compelling account of early telematic art, the social dimension of emerging technologies, and the enduring need for institutional support and public engagement.

Finally, the author explores the transformative role of new media art within the Venice Biennale's evolving curatorial structure, examining how technology introduced both creative potential and destabilising force into the traditional structure of the institution post-1968.

Biographical Note

Francesca Franco, PhD, is a UK and Italy-based curator, art historian and producer. She researches early computer art and its pioneers, with books including *Generative Systems Art* (2018), and *The Algorithmic Dimension* (2022). Notable curatorial projects include *Vera Molnár: Icône 2020* at the 59th Venice Biennale, *Algorithmic Signs* (Venice, 2017), and *Vera Molnár: Variazioni Icône* (Rome, 2023). She has commissioned significant new works, such as Molnár's first glasswork in Murano, *Icône* 2020 (2021), Roman Verostko's *St Mark's Apocalypse* (2017), and Ernest Edmonds's *Growth and Form* (2017). She is Visiting Professor at KIT Karlsruhe Institute of Technology and 2025 SIGGRAPH Art Gallery Chair.

References

Lawrence Alloway, *The Venice Biennale, 1895–1968; from Salon to Goldfish Bowl*, Faber & Faber, London 1969.

Francesca Franco, "The First Computer Art Show at the 1970 Venice Biennale. An Experiment or Product of the Bourgeois Culture?" in *Relive – Media Art Histories*, Cubitt, S., and Thomas, P. (Eds.), Cambridge, Mass.: The MIT Press, 2013, 119–134.

Adrian Searle, theguardian.com, Friday 31 May 2013, online at http://www.theguardian.com/artanddesign/2013/may/31/prada-venice-biennale-2013, accessed on 20 August 2013.

It Was Meant 2 b gr8: Reneging on the Participatory Ethos of Software Culture in the 2003 Venice Biennale

Simon Pope

In December 2002 I was invited to take part in Wale's first exhibition at the Venice Biennale of Fine Art 2003, along with three other artists: Cerith Wyn-Evans, Bethan Huws, and Paul Seawright. Patricia Fleming, a Glasgow-based curator, selected artists who had complex relationships with Wales as a nation state, and I was included in the roster as an emerging artist, with English as a first language, and who was embroiled in networked cultures locally and internationally. My recent work had included a curatorial project that influenced both the work that I produced in Venice and how I understood my relationship as a new media artist to other contemporary artists.

Art for Networks started as a co-production with BBC Wales and BBC Online in London: a series of artists' talks at Chapter, a contemporary art gallery in Cardiff, UK, in 2000–01 by net.artists and others associated with networked approaches to art practice, complimented by interviews by Matthew Fuller, a colleague in the net. art collective I/O/D. This was followed by a national touring exhibition, funded by Arts Council England and the Henry Moore Foundation, and organized by Chapter, who published the exhibition catalogue (Pope and Firth 2002)—and were revenue-funded by Arts Council Wales. The proposal to Arts Council England explicitly made the link between the work of net.artists—including Heath Bunting, Rachel Baker, and JODI— and other contemporary artists—such as Adam Chodzko and Stephen Willats, Anna Best and Ryosuke Cohen—who shared their preoccupations with social relations and social networks. This project came to fruition as Nicolas Bourriaud's "Esthétique relationnelle" became widely available in English (Bourriaud 2002), and the "Relational Aesthetics" episode of the BBC arts

S. Pope (✉)
Centre for Rural Policy Research, University of Exeter, Exeter, UK
e-mail: S.Pope@exeter.ac.uk

F. Franco (ed.), *Computational Art at the Venice Biennale (1970–2015)*, Springer Series on Cultural Computing, https://doi.org/10.1007/978-3-032-04258-3_2

documentary *Art Safari* features a comical interview with me, trying to make sense of Bourriaud's work (without having yet read it)—but the producer/director/interviewer of the programme clearly recognized a confluence between my efforts and Bourriaud's more coherent and accomplished proposition (Lewis 2004). Beryl Graham was right when she guessed that I knew more about net.art and the legacy of conceptual art practice than "art where the public participates" (Corby 2013). Now, I would take issue with both her idea of participation and of the public, but then, Beryl was entirely right in her criticism. Not that I was unaware of theories of participation, however, but in the circles in which I moved at the time, participation was more thoroughly understood through *design* methodology (Helander et al. 1997), rather than as a form of "new genre-public art" (Lacy 1995); mine was an art practice that drew on the techniques of software engineering after all. But where Beryl *was* correct was when she suggested that this was a project that sought to establish a *hybrid* approach—that was its motivation and the trajectory that it traced, not only to suggest a wider affinities in contemporary and historical art practice but also as a diagnostic, speculative, generative process in my own practice. However, this was not meant to be a comprehensive overview and was, explicitly, my attempt to think through my own net.art practice, as a way to move towards other artists and peers. My work in Venice was a continuation of this personal project in many ways, as a means to bring me closer to the then-current discourse of contemporary art and its apparatuses. This confluence of net.art and less technically-defined contemporary art practices was a way towards what, for me, would eventually become an art practice understood in terms of the discourse of participatory, dialogic, and relational art that Beryl Graham recognized as absent in my earlier work.

The *Ambulant Science Studio* took its title from Deleuze and Guattari (1987), who suggest two modes of scientific practice: the *royal* and the *ambulant*. This latter mode, in contrast to the mathematical, geometrical, and "major" science, operates in a "minor" mode. A *poor* science, you might say, in the sense that *arte povera* gives us an *attitude, and an access to certain materials and processes,* which distinguished it from the "rich art" of Pop (Galimberti 2013). Working as part of the artists' collective I/O/D, I recognized that we were concerned with the same concepts as researchers working on large-scale corporate projects who we would often present alongside at new media conferences. The tools available to us were proprietorial (we used *Macromedia Director* and third-party plug-ins), pirated, and détourned from commercial projects, yet—through what I now consider an immense ingenuity and a sense of urgency—we were able to make software-as-art which rivalled upscale, bank-rolled software-as-engineering. I/O/D 4: *The Web Stalker* was the apotheosis of this. As self-proclaimed *speculative software* it laid bare the structural and formal qualities of the Web—as a hierarchical file structure on networked servers and as a symbolic-linking technology—left un-rendered in commercial Web browser software. It cost little to produce; it was given away "for free". With this software we restated the merits of the *poor* rather than the rich: "con poco o nulla" (Costantini 1976).

The Web Stalker, as all the other outputs by I/O/D—which initially took the form of multimedia publications—was made to be freely available and widely distributed. Initially, before we had access to electronic distribution, our work was copied to floppy disk—those that were rejected by a magazine company, who ordinarily attached disks to their glossy covers — and made them available to us free of charge. We would copy them by hand—in batches of 100 or so—affix a laser-printed and hand-cut label—and then hand them out to people we met, or who requested them. (I can remember giving Thomas Demand a copy of I/O/D #1, for example, when we met in Brixton High Street in the summer of 1993, after Lisa Haskel's gathering of new media artists and theorists at the ICA in London.) The ethos of copy-left, or anti-copyright was strong within the group, and by the time that I was making work in Venice, the culture of free software and Creative Commons licences was widely established. Between 1998 and 2001 I had also been collaborating with artist Mark Greco on *Ice Cream for Everyone* (2015). This project sought to break the proprietorial stranglehold of corporate ice cream manufacture, returning ice cream to "everyone" and anyone who wanted it. Again, ice cream was given away at art events—openings and exhibitions—and we had been invited to Open Culture academic conferences and to CRASH!—the group exhibition at the ICA in 2000. This work, although not electronic new media, or net.art, echoed the wider concerns of artists within those art worlds and networks. These approaches to art practice, to its production and distribution and ownership as understood within the discourse of media art at the time, and in software culture, and in the attempts to understand how this culture's influence would migrate to other disciplines and sectors, were direct influences on my work in Venice.

That the concept of the *ambulant* suggests a ground-level activity, a grassroots or tactical approach to media, to systems, or to living, echoed other concerns of mine at that time. In 2000, while working on a failed/abandoned social-network version of *The Web Stalker* with I/O/D, I write a popular (sic) technical manual, *London Walking* (Pope 2000). This book was published in the "manual" series by Ellipsis in London, alongside *The Manual: (How to Have a Number One the Easy Way)* by Jimmy Cauty and Bill Drummond of the KLF (1999) and a reprint of *Art and Social Function* by Stephen Willats (2000), which, I think, accurately describes several of the practices which were neighbours to my own at the time. My concern was to be *tactical*, rather than *strategic*, and to promote the vitality of grassroots and "poor" approaches: this was less of a Situationist-inspired overturning of the everyday through art, but perhaps a Kaprow-like transfer of everyday activity into art, though at the time I was more likely to have been thinking of Ted Nelson's *Xanadu* (1960), and the urgency of invention to think- and work-through an empirical problem: such as how to sustain a search for love. *Amora a Venezia* was a collection of photographs of prismatic diffraction of light through everyday things: glasses of Campari, plate-glass doors, kids' toy bubbles—seeing a rainbow as an indication of being in love. This theme continued in *Baci*, which was a scanned and enlarged laser-print of a map of Venice found in the *Ex birreria* exhibition space in Giudecca—the venue for the Wales pavilion. Mounted on a large, 4.5 m by 3 m free-standing board, a sign invited visitors to "mark with a 'x' wherever you have kissed", with a large stick of pink chalk. *Calendario Delle Maree* was a flotilla of origami gondolas made from the eponymous paper calendars available throughout the city. These were to be taken to the nearby Giudecca canal, to sense the depths of the water through watching its surface. A metaphorical exercise. *Lost in the Supermarket* took literally Marc Augé's claim that branded products orientate visitors in airports and other "non-places". Sceptical of this, I produced a model of Venice from products, familiar to me from the UK, but bought in a nearby supermarket on the Zattere, which mimicked the techniques outlined in Kevin Lynch's influential *Image of the City* (1960), mapping landmarks and illustrating a mental map to aid navigation. *Stones of Venice*—an obvious pun—was a hoard of granite paving-setts, which were used everywhere across the city, and indeed across Europe at that time, as part of a wave of urban regeneration at the turn of the millennium. These were arranged in a rough approximation of Piazza San Marco and ordered according to how far I might be able to throw them, as ammo, if called upon to do so. Again, metaphors abound. A video, never exhibited, records me weighing and placing each stone, as I'd seen workers in the street doing as they laid the new paving. In the audio work, *Whistle Test*, I learned the technique for communicating from the shore to nearby boats using the Venetian vernacular: a sharp whistle.

These "devices" that I produced in Venice were small-scale, hand-made, do-it-yourself attempts at making sense of the locale, for preparing for certain eventualities, and for calling for their deployment by other people. They drew on the instructional format of *London Walking*—itself partly influenced by Yoko Ono's *Grapefruit* (1964), which was reprinted around that time (Ono 2000). And so they were idiosyncratic, of my own invention, rather than developed through a participatory process—in the sense of being developed with others.

Although I had written a polemical text called *Art Is Everything, Business Is Not* for Arts Council England in 2002 (White et al. 2002), in which I called for the separation of art from business, I did not fully acknowledge this in my work in Venice. As well as calling for a retreat from the more mercantile aspects of the art world—its dealers, collectors, and so on—I was also preoccupied with maintaining a distance from the "discount" research and development that artists perform, especially in the realm of software and, at the time, for example, "enhanced reality" gaming. I was also well aware of artists' implication in wider neoliberal projects of deregulation through the disruption to existing markets by technological innovation; and the members of I/O/D were aware of, but addressed only subsequently, the implication of artists within a wider project—the *Californian Ideology* of Barbrook and Cameron (1995)—which we now see flourishing in the "Uberisation" of everything (Kaye 2015). Not only were artists the shock-troops of urban regeneration/revitalization/gentrification—core constituents of Richard Florida's "creative class" (Florida 2003)—they were also in-league with a new generation of de-regulators, modelling business as "tactical media" and subaltern art projects in order to break unions, break regulations, and set legal precedent: Taxis now, healthcare later, to paraphrase one silicon valley venture capitalist (Basan 2015). I/O/D's five-word Webby Awards acceptance speech in 2000 proclaimed, "Technical innovation equals class war" (Webby Awards 2015). What we did not foresee at the time was that this war would be waged on us, and by a class other than our own.

I/O/D eventually disbanded with one of its members pursuing a career as a commercial software programmer, with the others moving towards art and the academy. Although we were not directly influenced by the *Experiments in Art and Technology* and its *9 Evenings* events of 1966, ours was an art practice that followed the route, as Stuart Hobbs indicates, into "the university model of technical specialisation", typical of American avant-garde art practice, and which "provided a better model for artistic exploration than the avant-garde model of *épater le bourgeois*" (Hobbs 1997).

The Ambulant Science Studio was developed in the first year of my NESTA Fellowship award, which provided me with the pretext to explore, over the course of three years, extra-institutional approaches to research and development that would ordinarily be undertaken within a corporate or academic context. The work was, in that sense, an informal approach to research, informed by my attempts, as a member of I/O/D, to develop a do-it-yourself approach, grappling with technical problems that were otherwise the privileged domain of IBM or Google R&D labs. The "devices" that I invented for the project in Venice were developed rapidly and iteratively; they were distributed "for free" and retained a punk or garage band ethos. But this approach left me vulnerable, I think, to criticisms of not taking the project seriously, of playing around with street politics to little or no effect, and without the investment of time and the building of personal and social relationships that would make this work transformative in its effect. My attempts at bringing these software-culture-derived ways of working into a contemporary art context were perhaps ill-timed and ill-fated. I could never have spectacularized my work—no data projections, no motion-capture suits, no green screens—but I could have paid more attention to the collaborative or participatory working practices that I had grown into through my software culture work. A retreat into idiosyncratic, and fundamentally "lone working" worked against the ethos of that culture—an ethos that I have since taken to heart, and which—again—motivates my current practice.

One of the hand-made t-shirts that I wore throughout the project—printed with text-message-style adaptations of slogans from London post-Situationists, *King Mob*—perhaps sums up my experience of Venice most succinctly: "It was meant 2 b gr8 but it's horrible" (Pope 2003). Next time I will go along mob-handed.

Biographical Note

Simon Pope's (b. 1966, Exeter, UK) art practice has been preoccupied with art and networks, the socialities of walking, more-than-human social worlds and – most recently – in the practice of football. Formerly a member of the Net.Art group I/O/D, he represented Wales at the Venice Biennale in 2003. Pope was a NESTA Fellowship awardee (2002–05), a Reader in Fine Art (2005–10), and holds a DPhil in Fine Art from The Ruskin School of Art, University of Oxford (2012-15). He is currently a Research Associate at the Centre for Rural Policy Research at The University of Exeter and a supervisor for Transart Institute's PhD programme. More information at: https://simonpope.info

References

"THE CALIFORNIAN IDEOLOGY by Richard Barbrook and Andy Cameron I Imaginary Futures," 1995, http://www.imaginaryfutures.net/2007/04/17/the-californian-ideology-2/.

Ira Basan, "In the Valley of the Kings," *The Sunday Edition* (cbc, February 22, 2015), http://www.cbc.ca/radio/thesundayedition/the-niqab-and-citizenship-the-bystander-effect-train-love-in-the-valley-of-the-kings-1.2963290/in-the-valley-of-the-kings-an-ira-basen-documentary-1.2963565.

Nicolas Bourriaud, *Relational Aesthetics* (Presses du réel, 2002).

Jimmy Cauty and Bill Drummond, *The Manual: (How to Have a Number One the Easy Way)* (Ellipsis, 1999).

Tom Corby, *Network Art: Practices and Positions* (Routledge, 2013), 45.

C. Costantini, *Con poco o nulla: ricette di cucina popolare toscana* (Libreria editrice fiorentina, 1976).

Gilles Deleuze and Félix Guattari, *A Thousand Plateaus: Capitalism and Schizophrenia*, trans. Brian Massumi, 1st edition (Minneapolis: University of Minnesota Press, 1987), 372.

Richard Florida, *The Rise of the Creative Class: And How It's Transforming Work, Leisure, Community, and Everyday Life* (Basic Books, 2003).

Jacopo Galimberti, "A Third-Worldist Art? Germano Celant's Invention of *Arte Povera*," *Art History* 36, no. 2 (April 2013): 421, doi:https://doi.org/10.1111/j.1467-8365.12006.x.

Mark Greco, "Ice Cream for Everyone," accessed August 26, 2015, http://bak.spc.org/ice/.

M. G. Helander, T. K. Landauer, and P. V. Prabhu, *Handbook of Human-Computer Interaction* (Elsevier, 1997), 256–296.

Stuart D. Hobbs, *The End of the American Avant Garde: American Social Experience Series* (NYU Press, 1997).

Jonathan Kaye, "Uber v. Taxi," *The Walrus*, 2015, http://thewalrus.ca/uber-v-taxi/.

Suzanne Lacy, *Mapping the Terrain: New Genre Public Art* (Seattle: Bay Press, 1995).

Ben Lewis, "Art Safari—Relational Art: Is It An Ism?," TV Broadcast, *Art Safari* (BBC 4, 2004), http://www.ubu.com/film/relational.html.

Kevin A. Lynch, *The Image of the City* (Cambridge Mass: MIT, 1960).

Ted Nelson, "Project Xanadu®," 1960, http://www.xanadu.com/.

Yoko Ono, *Grapefruit: A Book of Instructions and Drawings* (New York: Simon & Schuster Ltd, 2000).

Simon Pope, *London Walking: A Handbook for Survival* (London [England]: Ellipsis, 2000).

Simon Pope, *It Was Meant 2 B gr8 but It's horrible*, t-shirt, 2003, http://41.media.tumblr.com/aba614ea5dffc9973f69b4621e4e7272/tumblr_nsxswcqpU51u5fpdio4_250.jpg

Simon Pope and Hannah Firth, *Art for Networks* (Cardiff: Chapter, 2002), http://catalogue.sunderland.ac.uk/items/153241.

Webby Awards, http://www.webbyawards.com/press/speeches/web-Stalker-Technical-Innovation-Equals-Class-War/, accessed August 18, 2015, http://www.webbyawards.com/post_5_word_speeches.xml.

Tony White et al., "Ways of Working [electronic Resource]: Placing Artists in Business Contexts" (Arts Council of England, 2002).

Stephen Willats, *Art and Social Function* (Ellipsis, 2000).

Site Venice Site Biennale: The Manifest.AR Augmented Reality Intervention into the 2011 Venice Biennale

Tamiko Thiel

Introduction

In 2011, using geolocative augmented reality (AR), the author was the primary organizer of the Manifest.AR cyberartist group intervention into the Venice Art Biennale, together with fellow artists Sander Veenhof and Mark Skwarek (Manifest. AR Venice Biennale Manifesto 2013). Using GPS coordinates we placed virtual artworks—visible in smartphone displays as overlays on the live camera view of the surroundings—inside the curatorially closed spaces of the Biennale.

Unlike physical interventions, the artworks cannot be removed or blocked by authorities. The artworks exploit the site as their canvas while simultaneously questioning the value of location, and the power of the curator as gatekeeper, to canonize works of art.

The Venice Biennale, founded in 1895, is the world's oldest art biennale and the city's main claim to relevance as a contemporary art destination. In the intervention we wished to question the biennale system, and the art world's use of that system to define artistic value, but also address the site as artists: the reality of Venice's contemporary concerns and of life in the city today.

Reprinted from AR[t] magazine, Royal Academy of Art AR Lab/The Hague, May 2014, issue 5, pages 56–65.

T. Thiel (✉)
Munich, Germany
e-mail: tamiko@alum.mit.edu

F. Franco (ed.), *Computational Art at the Venice Biennale (1970–2015)*, Springer Series on Cultural Computing, https://doi.org/10.1007/978-3-032-04258-3_3

Challenging and Exploiting the Primacy of Site

Manifest.AR (Manifest.AR AR Art Manifesto 2011) originally formed around an AR intervention into the United States' most iconic contemporary art space: the Museum of Modern Art in New York. In 2010 Sander Veenhof and Mark Skwarek realized that the institutional walls of the white cube were no longer solid, and organized a guerilla exhibit of augmented reality artworks inside the walls of MoMA.[1]

Since time immemorial location has been used to consecrate objects and people. In the art world too, access to a location—a gallery, a museum or other curatorially closed space—is tightly controlled to confer value and thus, via this exclusivity, to canonize the works shown there as "high art." What does it mean however to control physical space when in geolocated virtual space anyone can place whatever they want? (Aceti 2008).

Technically, it is a trivial difference in GPS coordinates that moves a virtual object from a public space such as Central Park to the curatorially closed space inside the sacred walls of MoMA. The epiphany of AR however is that although the artworks are virtual, their presence at the site is real, "actually existing as a thing or occurring in fact; not imagined or supposed" (Oxford English Dictionary 2013), reproducible by anyone who views the artwork at that location. In this "consensual hallucination," that was the dream of the early cyberpunk authors and virtual reality evangelists (Gibson 1984), augmented reality redefines the barriers between "the real" and "the virtual."

The artworks engage viewers with the site physically as well. Like bird watchers with binoculars, AR viewers scan their surroundings with their smartphones, dodging real world obstacles in search of the artwork, situating themselves and the act of viewing in their physical experience of that site.

Artistically, our works often stand in dialogue with the "official" artworks at a venue, and with the curator's theme and concept—with the visual presence of our artworks at the site increasing the potency of their argument.[2] In a time when many question the relevance of galleries, museums and biennales as venues for art, we save the gated communities of the art world from irrelevance by bringing a new form of dialogue into their institutions (Fidel 2010).

[1] "We AR in MoMA" (Veenhof 2010) was part of the Conflux Festival of Psychogeography (Conflux Festival 2010). Cyberpunk author Bruce Sterling blogged the intervention on WIRED (Sterling 2010), MoMA tweeted a somewhat nonplussed acknowledgment (MoMA 2010), and in a New York Times interview MoMA's director of digital media welcomed our engagement (Fidel 2010).

[2] The author's contribution to "We AR in MoMA" was a matrix of screaming faces titled "ARt Critic Face Matrix," a self-referential artwork that critiqued its own validity as an artwork, reflecting on the role of MoMA NY to define what did or did not constituted art (Thiel 2010).

Manifest.AR Venice Biennale Intervention: Themes and Concerns

At the 2011 Venice Biennale we wished to reflect not on Venice's past glory, but on its current condition: not only wrestling with climate change and overrun by tourists, but also fighting for relevance in the art world. The national pavilions that dominate the Venice Biennale reflect its origins at the end of the nineteenth century and the rise of the nation-state with a presumed monolithic ethnic or cultural identity. They stand now in direct contrast to the globalized, itinerant world of contemporary artists and their multiple systems of cultural reference (Madra 2006).

Curator Bice Curiger's opening statement questioned this structure as well: "By adopting the title ILLUMInations the 54th International Art Exhibition of the Venice Biennale also aspires literally to shed light on the institution itself, drawing attention to dormant and unrecognized opportunities, as well as to conventions that need to be challenged... Far removed from culturally conservative constructs of 'nation,' art offers the potential to explore new forms of 'community' and negotiate differences and affinities that might serve as models for the future" (Curiger 2011). Curiger also posed five questions on identity to each of the artists officially included in the Biennale: "Where do you feel at home? Does the future speak English or another language? Is the artistic community a nation? How many nations do you feel inside yourself? If art was a nation what would be written in its constitution?"[3]

As an international artist collective that coalesced around challenging conventions of inclusion and participation, we saw this as a personal invitation to participate. Sander hijacked Curiger's curatorial statement and the Venice Biennale website to create our Venice Manifesto, in which we proclaimed:

As "one of the world's most important forums for the dissemination and 'illumination' about the current developments in international art" the 54th Biennale of Venice could not justify its reputation without an uninvited Manifest.AR Augmented Reality infiltration. In order to "challenge the conventions through which contemporary art is viewed" we have constructed virtual AR pavilions directly amongst the 30-odd buildings of the lucky few within the Giardini. In accordance with the "ILLUMInations" theme and Bice Curiger's five questions our uninvited participation will not be bound by nation-state borders, by physical boundaries or by conventional art world structures. The AR pavilions at the 54th Biennale reflect on a rapidly expanding and developing new realm of Augmented Reality Art that radically crosses dimensional, physical and hierarchical boundaries (Manifest.AR Venice Biennale Manifesto 2011) (Fig. 1).

Questions about control of space are not confined to art venues; "public" art is always dependent on permissions from authorities, and many a "public" space is actually closely controlled. We therefore placed our artworks not only in the controlled curatorial space of the Venice Giardini, but also in the public space of Piazza

[3]Although Curiger refers frequently to the "five questions," they are not to be found on the official Venice Biennale website. See however Flash Art (2011).

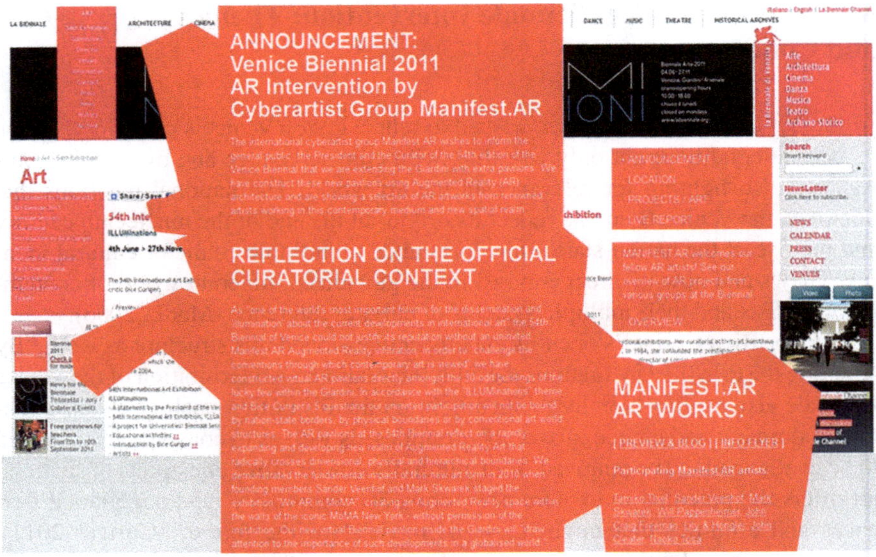

Fig. 1 Manifest.AR Venice Biennale Intervention website

San Marco, which has itself seen censorship of officially planned artworks (Magill 2007).

Manifest.AR Artworks in the Venice Biennale Intervention

Tamiko Thiel's ***Shades of Absence*** is a series of three "virtual pavilions" in the Giardini, in Piazza San Marco and inside the German National Pavilion. Anonymized golden silhouettes of artists whose works have been censored are enclosed by terms of censorship. In reply to Bice Curiger's questions: "Is the artistic community a nation? If art was a nation what would be written in its constitution?" they posit a transnational community of censored artists. Touching the artworks in the display of a smartphone calls up a website with cases of censorship (Thiel 2011) (Fig. 2).

Sander Veenhof's ***Battling Pavilions*** directly addresses the role of the curator, the exclusivity of the Giardini and the limited number of national pavilions allowed within its Sacred Grove. Users outside the Giardini can subvert Curiger's authority and create new virtual pavilions for nations of their choice inside the Giardini. Users inside the Giardini, in contrast, can help Curiger defend the Giardini against intruding pavilions by deleting them. In a classic twist, Sander's intervention also became an official part of the Biennale: dropstuff.nl invited him to show his Battling Pavilions on their large screens in three locations around Venice (Veenhof 2011) (Fig. 3).

Fig. 2 ***Shades of Absence: Public Voids***, Tamiko Thiel, Piazza San Marco

Fig. 3 ***Battling Pavilions***, Sander Veenhof, Venice

Mark Skwarek's ***Island of Hope*** addresses the perpetual threat of Venice sinking into the lagoon. Skwarek posits new forces of continental uplift erupting as fully formed baroque gardens into the Giardini and in Piazza San Marco. The islands are full of objects of hope, and tweets with the hash tag #hope, in order to bring hope back to Venice (Skwarek 2011) (Fig. 4).

John Craig Freeman's ***Water wARs: Squatters Pavilion*** is a virtual squatter's camp for refugees of water wars, one inside the protecting walls of the Giardini, and another "public" camp in Piazza San Marco. In Venice, a city founded by refugees and threatened by constant flooding, Water wARs calls attention to the escalating global struggle for this basic human need. It questions the ability of sovereign nations to isolate themselves from the rest of the world, as worldwide ecological disasters drive people in desperation to violate the boundaries of the nation-states in pursuit of sheer survival (Freeman 2011) (Fig. 5).

In John Cleater's ***Sky Pavilions*** ships from outer space take over Venice: The mothership hovers over Piazza San Marco emitting a mixture of nonsense and guidance to confuse and help tourists, natives, and art seekers. In the Giardini alien "Floaties" lie in wait, begging to be touched, and when activated by obliging visitors spin upwards, carrying secret messages to the mother ship. Sky Pavilions goes beyond the concept of the nation-state, beyond the concerns of mere earthbound humanoids and reminds us that the last word in the control of space may not be ours to decide (Cleater 2011) (Fig. 6).

Lily and Honglei's ***The Crystal Coffin: Virtual China Pavilion*** is inspired by China's petrified symbol of eternal Party rule, Mao Zedong's crystal coffin. In the Giardini it questions the traditional hierarchy of privilege among national pavilions in the Biennale and thematizes the rise of China as an important center of contemporary art. Another pavilion in Piazza San Marco dominates the heart of Venice, whose native son Marco Polo "discovered" China for the West, with this symbol of Chinese Party power (Lily and HongLei 2011) (Fig. 7).

Fig. 4 ***The Island of Hope***, Mark Skwarek, Venice Giardini

Fig. 5 ***Water wARs, Giardini***, John Craig Freeman, Venice Giardini

Will Pappenheimer/Virta-Flaneurazine's ***Colony Illuminati*** appropriated both the Biennale title "ILLUMInations" and the actual visual imagery of many artworks in the Biennale. A secret colony of virtual bufo toads draws sustenance from high art; as a form of camouflage their skins appropriate imagery from artworks around them in the Giardini and spread out into the city, seeking the outlying venues of the Venice Biennale. When touched on the smartphone screen, the toads release psychotropic drugs that trigger hallucinations in the viewer: a swirl of Internet information on the Biennale and waves of Tintorettoesque ecstasy that Curiger proclaimed to be the true essence of ILLUMInations (Pappenheimer/Virta-Flaneurazine 2011) (Fig. 8).

Naoko Tosa's ***Historia*** addresses Curiger's question "Does the future speak English or another language?" and her view that "art offers the potential to explore new forms of 'community' and negotiate differences and affinities that might serve as models for the future." Historia appropriates iconic images from all nations and world cultures, modern and ancient, and allows visitors to arrange them in sequences, assigning them new meanings. It thus playfully examines the process by which artists appropriate and redefine existing cultural symbols to create their own individual languages (Tosa 2011) (Fig. 9).

I end with a quotation from Bice Curiger's curatorial text for the Venice Biennale:

> ILLUMInations presents contemporary art characterized by gestures that explore notions of the collective, yet also speak of fragmentary identity, of temporary alliances, and objects inscribed with transience. If the communicative aspect is crucial to the ideas underlying ILLUMInations, it is demonstrated in art that often declares and seeks closeness to the vibrancy of life. This is more important now than ever before, in an age when our sense of

Fig. 6 ***Sky Pavilions***, John Cleater, Piazza San Marco

Fig. 7 ***The Crystal Coffin***, Lily and Honglei, Piazza San Marco

Fig. 8 ***Colony Illuminati***, Will Pappenheimer/Virta-Flaneurazine, Venice Giardini

Fig. 9 ***Historia***, Naoko Tosa, Venice Giardini

> reality is profoundly challenged by virtual and simulated worlds. This Biennale is also about believing in art and its potential. (Curiger 2011)

I could not agree more. Perhaps in ways that Bice Curiger did not anticipate.

Coda: The Future of AR Interventions

At the latest since the Salon des Refusés in 1863, questions about the validity of the art canon and the institutions that define this canon have been an important part of the evolution of modern art. Augmented reality interventions are the continuation of this modernist dialogue with twenty-first century means.

But how will the law react to increasing transgressions in virtual space? By 2013 technologies such as Google's Street View and Glass were provoking wide public discussion of the confluence of locative, mobile, recording and display technologies, and what negative effects could come of the blurring of boundaries between real and virtual space. Most public unease comes however not from AR display technology, but from recording ("surveillance") technology. As Yolande Kolstee points out, the real debate here is not technological but social, and can probably be negotiated using existing legislation (Kolstee 2013).

Can institutions use these existing laws to assert "virtual air rights" to "their" GPS coordinates, thus blocking AR interventions? Intellectual property lawyer Brian Wassom thinks not: "Property law is about the right to exclude others from physical space. But an infinite number of people can each create their own AR layer superimposing digital data over the same physical space without impeding anyone else's ability to do so, and without invading the rights of the real property owner" (Wassom 2014).

Biographical Note

Tamiko Thiel is an internationally known visual artist exploring the interplay of place, space, the body and cultural memory. She is a founding member of Manifest. AR, participating in 2010 in their pathbreaking augmented reality intervention at MoMA NY, and being the main curator and organizer of their 2011 AR intervention at the Venice Biennale.

Her works are featured in the reference books Digital Art (Thames and Hudson World of Art, by Whitney Museum curator Christiane Paul—includes her Venice Biennale intervention), Augmented Reality Art (Vladimir Geroimenko, ed.), The World of Digital Art (DAM director Wolf Lieser) and "Not Here Not There" special AR issue of Leonardo Electronic Almanac (Aceti, Rinehart & Sahin, ed.)

Her grants and fellowships include the MacDowell Colony, WIRED Magazine, Japan Foundation, MIT, Berlin Capital City Cultural Fund (Hauptstadtkulturfonds), Goethe-Institut, IBM Innovation Award for Art and Technology, FACT Liverpool and Zero1 Biennale. She is also augmented reality artistic advisor for the Caribbean Cultural Center and African Diaspora Institute's augmented reality project in Spanish Harlem, NY, for which she helped bring in a Rockefeller Foundation Cultural Innovation Award.

Her guest professorships include Carnegie-Mellon University, UC/San Diego, Bauhaus-University Weimar, the Berlin University of the Arts and Nanyang Technological University Singapore.

References

Aceti L (2008) The Virtual Places We Own: When Communities and Artists Occupy Your Place without Your Consent. Internet Research 9.0: Rethinking Community, Rethinking Place: 15–18

Cleater J (2011) Sky Pavilions. Manifest.AR Venice Biennale 2011 Intervention website. http://manifestarblog.wordpress.com/cleater-venice-2011/. Accessed 14 March 2013

Conflux Festival (2010) We AR in MoMA. http://confluxfestival.org/projects/conflux-festival-2010/we-ar-in-moma/. Accessed 30 April 2012

Curiger B (2011) Introduction by Bice Curiger. ILLUMInazioni—ILLUMInations. Venice Biennale website. http://www.labiennale.org/en/art/archive/54th-exhibition/curiger/. Accessed 12 March 2013

Fidel A (2010, December 1) Art Gets Unmasked in the Palm of Your Hand. New York Times http://www.nytimes.com/2010/12/02/arts/02iht-rartsmart.html. Accessed 30 April 2012

Flash Art (2011) Bice Curiger speaks about the Venice Biennale. http://www.flashartonline.com/interno.php?pagina=news_det&id=953&det=ok&title=Bice-Curiger-speaks-about-the-Venice-Biennale. Accessed 12 March 2013

Freeman JC (2011) Water wARs: Squatters Pavilion. Manifest.AR Venice Biennale 2011 Intervention website. http://manifestarblog.wordpress.com/freeman-venice-2011/. Accessed 14 March 2013

Gibson W (1984) Neuromancer. Ace Books, New York.
Kolstee Y (2013) Who owns the space? AR[t] Issue 3, November 2013, http://arlab.nl/artmagazine/art-magazine-issue-3-online. Accessed 7 April 2014.
Lily and Honglei (2011) The Crystal Coffin: Virtual China Pavilion. Manifest.AR Venice Biennale 2011 Intervention website. http://manifestarblog.wordpress.com/lily-honglei-venice-2011/. Accessed 14 March 2013
Madra Y (2006) From Imperialism to Transnational Capitalism: The Venice Biennial as a 'Transitional Conjuncture.' Rethinking Marxism 18(4). http://www.academia.edu/2072820/From_Imperialism_to_Transnational_Capitalism_The_Venice_Biennial_as_a_Transitional_Conjuncture_. Accessed 14 March 2013
Magill R J Jr (2007, 16 April) For Gregor Schneider's cube, a long pilgrimage. New York Times. http://www.nytimes.com/2007/04/16/arts/16iht-cube.1.5303319.html. Accessed 14 March 2013
Manifest.AR AR Art Manifesto (2011, 25 January). Manifest.AR artist group official website. http://www.manifestar.info/. Accessed 12 March 2013
Manifest.AR Blog (2013) About Manifest.AR. http://manifestarblog.wordpress.com/about/. Accessed 12 March 2013
Manifest.AR Venice Biennale Manifesto (2011, 25 January) Venice Biennial 2011 AR Intervention by Cyberartist Group Manifest.AR, Reflection on the official curatorial context. http://www.manifestar.info/venicebiennial2011/. To view the actual artworks in Venice go to the launch page—only accessible on mobile devices: http://manifestar.info/vb11/. (Both accessed 14 March 2013).
MoMa (Museum of Modern Art) NY Twitter site (2010, 8 October). Nice, looks like we're having an "uninvited" AR exhibition tomorrow! Part of @confluxfestival. https://twitter.com/#!/MuseumModernArt/statuses/26786135774. Accessed 12 March 2013
Oxford English Dictionary. Definition of "real." http://oxforddictionaries.com/us/definition/american_english/real. Accessed 12 March 2013
Pappenheimer W, Virta-Flaneurazine (2011) Colony Illuminati. Manifest.AR Venice Biennale 2011 Intervention. http://manifestarblog.wordpress.com/pappenheimer-venice-2011/. Accessed 12 March 2013
Skwarek M (2011) Parade to Hope. Manifest.AR Venice Biennale 2011 Intervention. http://manifestarblog.wordpress.com/skwarek-venice-2011/. Accessed 12 March 2013
Sterling B (2010, 6 October) Augmented Reality: AR uninvited at MOMA NYC. Beyond the Beyond. WIRED. http://www.wired.com/beyond_the_beyond/2010/10/augmented-reality-ar-uninvited-at-moma-nyc. Accessed 30 April 2012
Thiel T (2010, October) We AR in MoMA exhibit. Tamiko Thiel website. http://mission-base.com/tamiko/We-AR-in-MoMA/. Accessed 12 March 2013
Thiel T (2011, May) Shades of Absence. Manifest.AR Venice Biennale 2011 Intervention. http://manifestarblog.wordpress.com/thiel_venice-2011/. Accessed 12 March 2013
Tosa N (2011) Historia. Manifest.AR Venice Biennale 2011 Intervention. http://manifestarblog.wordpress.com/naoko-tosa-venice-biennial-2011/. Accessed 30 April 2012
Veenhof S (2010, 9 October) DIY day MoMA Oct 9th 2010 AUGMENTED REALITY art invasion! Sander Veenhof website. http://www.sndrv.nl/moma/. Accessed 12 March 2013
Veenhof S (2011) Battling Pavilions. Manifest.AR Venice Biennale 2011 Intervention. http://manifestarblog.wordpress.com/sander-veenhof-venice-biennial-2011/. See also: http://www.sndrv.nl/battle/. Accessed 14 March 2013
Wassom B (2014) Augmented Reality as Free Speech. Augmented Legality blog. http://www.wassom.com/from-the-archives-augmented-reality-as-free-speech.html. Accessed 2 April 2014

vOluptuary drOid décOlletage at the 55th International Art Exhibition of la Biennale di Venezia

Joseph Nechvatal

In the beginning was the noise.

—Michele Serres, The Parasite

Joseph Nechvatal, *vOluptuary drOid décOlletage*, 168 × 305 cm, 2002, exhibition view, *Noise*, collateral event of the 55th International Art Exhibition of la Biennale di Venezia: Il Palazzo Enciclopedico. (Courtesy: Galerie Richard Paris/New York)

J. Nechvatal (✉)
Magenta Plains, New York City, NY, USA
e-mail: jnech@thing.net

F. Franco (ed.), *Computational Art at the Venice Biennale (1970–2015)*, Springer Series on Cultural Computing, https://doi.org/10.1007/978-3-032-04258-3_4

I would like to explain a bit of how *vOluptuary drOid décOlletage* functioned for me at the 55th International Art Exhibition of la Biennale di Venezia while simultaneously promoting the aesthetics of obscurity.

Recently in my book *Immersion Into Noise* (Nechvatal 2011) I have mapped out a broad spectrum of aesthetic activity I call the *art of noise* by tracing its past eruptions where figure/ground merge and flip the common emphasis to some extent. *Immersion Into Noise* concludes with a look at the figural aspect of this aesthetic lodged within the ground of consciousness itself.[1] For me, the obscurity of *vOluptuary drOid décOlletage* exemplifies well a general noise aesthetic needed now within our broad-spectrum data-monitoring info-economy environment of background machine-to-machine gigabyte communication murmur[2] in which we now find ourselves. *vOluptuary drOid décOlletage* is a good example of the speculative reality of noise aesthetics in our era of algorithmic globalization.

The following reflection on *vOluptuary drOid décOlletage* at the 55th International Art Exhibition of la Biennale di Venezia is somewhat of a reaction to what some interesting contemporary philosophers have been saying about contemporary art. Most notably, the surprising talk *The Next Avant-Garde* that the philosopher Graham Harman gave at the *Aesthetics in the 21st Century* Conference at the University of Basel in September 2012 that engaged me with the recent *speculative realism*[3] turn in continental philosophy and aesthetics. In that talk Harman criticizes Relational Art,[4] calling it convivial art, so as to circle back to the formalist, media-specific aesthetics of the art critic Clement Greenberg, where art objects are free of the "tyranny of context." This supposed context freedom merges efficiently with Harman's theory of Object-Oriented Ontology[5] (OOO) but seemed somewhat at

[1] This involves a question of the qualities (and levels) of awareness of our own consciousness within aesthetic realms which we are capable of attaining through noise art (Nechvatal 2011, p. 210).

[2] Stupendous amounts of data generated by nearly 1 billion people are set in motion each day as, with an innocuous click or tap, people download movies on iTunes, check credit card balances through Visa's Web site, send e-mail with files attached, buy products, post on Twitter, or read newspapers and art theory papers online.

[3] Speculative realism is a movement in contemporary philosophy which defines itself loosely in its stance of metaphysical realism against the dominant forms of post-Kantian philosophy or what it terms correlationism. While often in disagreement over basic philosophical issues, the speculative realist thinkers have a shared resistance to philosophies of human finitude inspired by the tradition of Immanuel Kant.

[4] Relational art or relational aesthetics is a mode or tendency in fine art practice originally observed and highlighted by French art critic Nicolas Bourriaud. Bourriaud defined the approach simply as a set of artistic practices which take as their theoretical and practical point of departure the whole of human relations and their social context, rather than an independent and private space. The artist can be more accurately viewed as the "catalyst" in relational art, rather than being at the center.

[5] Object-oriented ontology (OOO) is a metaphysical movement that rejects the privileging of human existence over the existence of nonhuman objects. Specifically, object-oriented ontology opposes the anthropocentrism of Immanuel Kant's Copernican Revolution, whereby objects are said to conform to the mind of the subject and, in turn, become products of human cognition. In contrast to Kant's view, object-oriented philosophers maintain that objects exist independently of

odds with his proclaiming that "there must be a new avant-garde in every field" that we cannot predict. His call for a return to Greenbergian formalist, media-specific aesthetics, is hard to swallow whole as avant-garde. I mentioned to Harman, à propos, the irony of the intense dislike that Greenberg had for the late last work of Jackson Pollock, when Pollock went semi-representational, playing with indeterminate states of figure/ground ambiguity (for example, Jackson Pollock's portrait of Jane Smith, *No. 7* (1952) that I saw numerous times at her home, now owned by the Metropolitan Museum of Art).

Anyway, in the speech Harman touched on the subject of figure/ground relations[6] in the context of the anthropomorphic-free, flat ontology that emerged as part of the debates within the Speculative Realism movement. He coupled this figure/ground discussion with a Greenbergian medium-specific version of the Object-Oriented Ontology defense of an ontology of objects (rather than processes). This was a welcome tonic in a relational committed, but miserable, Europe of depressed post-convergent labor. His defense of objects amid the soaring (some would say souring) contemporary art trend of relations (deaesthetized and dematerialized) I found remarkable. Yet Harman failed to adequately account for the human singular (non-anthropomorphic-free) aspect involved in experiencing the art of noise, with its reversals in the order of figure/ground.

Without a rethinking of human singularity, I suggest that this omission conceals a concern for relational power, as we know from the life of Clement Greenberg. With the officially sanctioned support[7] and celebration of relational dematerialization, celeb-commodified into a brand and co-opted by the star-state-socio-economic system that is its life blood, the relational aesthetic[8] is no longer an idealized mode of art activity that (supposedly) accepts the full range of all human relations as art in opposition to private objects and spaces. That has pooped out, found often unsympathetically aloof: afloat within relational administrative systems of power.[9] The ideal of artistic exploration[10] of the full range of *all* human relations is clearly untenable at this administrative level—and obscure, singular human intimacy pays the price. The relational artist as catalyst[11] by means of flighty creations of intentionally

human perception and are not ontologically exhausted by their relations with humans or other objects.

[6] The main focus of my own noise art aesthetic theory.

[7] Curators promoting this "laboratory" paradigm include Maria Lind, Hans Ulrich Obrist, Barbara van der Linden, Hou Hanru, and Nicolas Bourriaud.

[8] Established by Nicolas Bourriaud, now director of the École Nationale Supérieure des Beaux-Arts in Paris.

[9] 2013 examples being Philippe Parreno's *Anywhere, anywhere out of the world* at the Palais de Tokyo, Pierre Huyghe's retrospective at Le Centre Pompidou, the Dia Art Foundation sponsored *Gramsci Monument* by Thomas Hirschhorn, and Tino Sehgal's win of the Golden Lion for the best artist in the *International Exhibition Il Palazzo Enciclopedico* in the Venice Biennale.

[10] Artists included by Bourriaud under the rubric of Relational Aesthetics include Rirkrit Tiravanija, Philippe Parreno, Carsten Höller, Henry Bond, Douglas Gordon, and Pierre Huyghe, among others.

[11] See "The Menagerie Entertains," my review of the Pierre Huyghe Retrospective at Le Centre Pompidou in *The Brooklyn Rail*, December 2013 Issue.

stuplime[12] works that fluctuate between sculpture, music, film clips, and small Fluxus-like events has turned the artist into a star-impresario-entrepreneur: a very specific, limiting, and quasi-domineering human relation. Coupled with fun-house-laboratory work based in an aesthetic paradigm of aloofness that is so cool it verges on cold, the relational art star is placed firmly back at the top-center of things and torn *away* from art that creates a social environment in which people come together to participate in a private-but-shared activity that is open-ended, interactive, and resistant to closure. Hirschhorn is the current exception to this relational bent.

With *vOluptuary drOid décOlletage* I will go on to make the case for a return to the art object as post-conceptually scalable and mutable (as opposed to art as process alone) that owes something to Harman's OOO object because the inherent detachment of work-in-progress post-medium practice, shorn of any deep commitment to medium specificity, seems to inscribe a limiting condition of superficiality on the artist while bestowing media success: a truly Mephistopheles-like metaphysical situation. One, Claire Bishop has suggested, that "seems to derive from a creative misreading of poststructuralist theory: rather than the interpretations of a work of art being open to continual reassessment, the work of art itself is argued to be in perpetual flux" (Bishop 2004).

Also, I have been following closely the public proclamations of another philosopher on art, Simon Critchley. Critchley described in 2010 contemporary art's dominant trend as an inauthenticity of "mannerist situationism" based in rituals of reenactment.[13] Critchley goes on in 2012 to describe the circumstances further, as the "cold mannerist obsessionality of the taste for appropriation and reenactment that has become hegemonic in the art world" (Critchley 2012). So things have gotten no better. Clearly something deep-seated must be reevaluated. And art aesthetics is more interesting when it does the work of shifting meaning. So I am declining here Critchley's urging for contemporary art to focus in on the *monstrous*, as, in my opinion, that parody of gloomy general dystopia only plays into the extreme spectacle aspect of mannerism. To be fair, Critchley doesn't explain what or who he means by the monstrous, but when I think of the monstrous today, I think of the high visibility of Lady Gaga (and her little monsters), extreme Hollywood lowbrow movies, and grotesque far right political claims and postures.

No, I am only interested in a new contemporary aesthetic labor based in the unseeablity of *vOluptuary drOid décOlletage*'s obscure *monster sacré* affinity for disconnectedness—one that focuses on an impregnable diva-like commitment to a nihilistic aesthetic of *becoming imperceptible.*[14] *vOluptuary drOid décOlletage* has

---

[12] In her chapter on "Stuplimity" from *Ugly Things*, Sianne Ngai offers this term as a necessary reaction to new, primarily postmodern, objects of analysis, a term that acknowledges stupidity and boredom as part of the sublime expression connected to the postmodern art experience.

[13] At his talk "The Faith of the Faithless, Experiments in Political Theology at the Dance Politics & Co-Immunity Workshop" in Giessen, Germany, November 12, 2010.

[14] "Although all becomings are already molecular, including becoming woman, it must be said that all becomings begin with and pass through becoming-woman. It is the key to all the other becomings. [...] If becoming- woman is the first quantum, or molecular segment, with the becomings-

an affinity with obscurity that takes you into embodied and embedded resonance perspectives, into radical immanence, and away from both pop imagery and pure abstraction. I am interested in an exquisite monster sacré aesthetic for *vOluptuary drOid décOlletage* where personal anthropomorphic eccentricities and indiscretions are tolerated by combining the neo-materialist[15] vibrant world with a wider vision of political awareness including private spiritual, ecstatic, or numinous themes accessible through the generative subjective realm of each individual; an aesthetics of perception-politics based on resonance (not a politics of visibility) which reveals in minute particulars the full spectrum of the extensive social-political dimensions.

This monster sacré affinity is a materialist nihilism of *ro* that (if it goes far enough) can transform a metamorphosis (subject to the flickering formative forces of emergence)[16] into an all-embracing *yes* of delicate abhorrence.[17] So I am advocating with *vOluptuary drOid décOlletage* not the passive and thus incomplete nihilism of form, but a generative and virulent and curative nihilism that unleashes forces of reverberation to emerge and resonate like a web of inter-connected, molecular and viral relational affects and intensities that traffics in dissonance, deviation, and the incidental.

But what specifically can we glean for art from this instability and resonance of covert nihilism? In what kind of regimes of attraction/repulsion can the resonant nihilistic art object participate, and what may it do differently from other signs and objects? To these questions I offer a counter-theory to OOO formalism—a theory of *à rebours*[18] exchanges of figure/ground relationships: a nimble art as monster sacré that emphasizes human and non-human entanglements. This is an art that depends on playing out nihilistic negativity by intensifying its forces into an affirmative nihilism. This nimble nihilist bracketing pushes the audience toward open defamiliarizations, challenging them to think outside of the normal system of human consciousness. In this way it is OOO aesthetically favorable. So this art as nimble monster sacré is implicated in the very type of problematic instability that the "self" undergoes in Nietzsche's thought: the cohesiveness of the culture/state distinction,

---

animal that link up with it coming next, what are they all rushing toward? Without a doubt, toward *becoming-imperceptible*. The imperceptible is the immanent end of becoming, its cosmic formula. […]" (Deleuze and Guattari 1987).

[15] Manuel DeLanda coined the term *neo-materialist* in a short 1996 text "The Geology of Morals, A Neo-Materialist Interpretation" where he treats a portion of Deleuze and Guattari's *A Thousand Plateaus* in order to conceptualize geological movements. For more on neo-materialist see Manuel DeLanda's interview in (2012).

[16] In philosophy, systems theory, science, and art, emergence is the way complex systems and patterns arise out of a multiplicity of relatively simple interactions. Emergence is central to the theories of integrative levels and of complex systems.

[17] For a musical comparison, see Hensley (2004).

[18] The meaning of *à rebours* is against the grain. Also, *À rebours* (1884) (translated as *Against Nature* or *Against the Grain*) is a decadent novel by the French writer Joris-Karl Huysmans. Its narrative concentrates on the tastes and inner life of Jean Des Esseintes, an eccentric, reclusive aesthete and antihero who loathes bourgeois society and tries to retreat into an ideal artistic world of his own creation.

like the cohesiveness of the "self/other" distinction, disintegrates with the ontological instability produced by the annihilation of the real as distinguishable from the illusory. With a nimble art of noise—based in the distinction between active nihilism and passive nihilism (or monstrous nihilism)—we can depict the underground vigor of form as an active verve that can only be speculated at by thinking beyond the discursive. And that enacts a shift away from the subject-object dualism that is currently much lauded by Object-Oriented Ontologists.

The embeddedness of our inner world—the life of our imagination with its intense drives, suspicions, fears, and loves—guides our intentions and actions in the political-economic world. Our inner world is the only true source of meaning and purpose we have, and nimble, exquisite gazing[19] (that involves self-investigation) is the way to discover for ourselves this inner life. So we might consider now that, in contrast to our frenzied data market surveillance culture,[20] that which trains us to fear the atrocious eyes of outer perception, a protracted and absorbing gazing at *vOluptuary drOid décOlletage* could encourage the development of agile clandestine exchanges based on the embedded individual intuitive eye in conjunctive contact with an abundant *optical-mnemonic commons* (not cloud)[21] that shares a sensibility for building a force. What I mean by optical-mnemonic commons is a visual memory of possible shared futures, a mnemonic gazing at that inter-subjective affinity which we share as the cooperative common ground of sociality: that shared common ground that precedes community. Such a commons of exchange is what has to be built politically through the creation of innovative individual-polis assemblages; new modes of organization of the individual-collective from which all could benefit.

Of course this sphere of anti-purist gazing-commons (essentially a cooperative rejection of the tyranny of labels, essential identities, privileged abstractions, and fixed ideas) is what allows art to construct unstable distinctions between subjects and objects that embrace the entire spectrum of imaginary spaces; from the infinitude of actual forms to formless voids of virtuality. Subsequently my interest here is in anti-pure nimble art like *vOluptuary drOid décOlletage* that challenges and

---

[19] *Gaze*; to look long and intently. *Gaze* is often indicative of wonder, fascination and revelation.

[20] For example take the blandly named Utah Data Center, built for the National Security Agency. A project of immense secrecy, it is the final piece in a complex puzzle assembled over the past decade. Its purpose: to intercept, decipher, analyze, and store vast swaths of the world's communications as they zap down from satellites and zip through the underground and undersea cables of international, foreign, and domestic networks. Flowing through its servers and routers and stored in near-bottomless databases will be all forms of communication, including the complete contents of private emails, cell phone calls, and Google searches, as well as all sorts of personal data trails—parking receipts, travel itineraries, bookstore purchases, and other digital transactions. It is, in some measure, the realization of the "total information awareness" program created during the first term of the Bush administration—an effort that was killed by Congress in 2003 after it caused an outcry over its potential for invading Americans' privacy. For more on this trend see Bamford's (2009).

[21] The term "cloud" is often generally used to describe a data center's functions. More specifically, it refers to a service for leasing computing capacity.

sometimes exchanges the hierarchy of figure and ground (figure and abstraction) through struggles with noise.[22]

Certainly globalization is all about world space, so noise art aesthetics here will continue to be thought of in terms of spatialization: dimensions, areas, and territories. What space does noise clear and what space does noise clog? How does noise function as an attractor for a gazing-commons and as a repellent in the monstrous era of global data mining and the digital surveillance state? How can monster sacré aesthetic thought help us to think and live differently within our smooth and surveyed spaces through art? How can we live more intently and intensely in our imaginary cosmos of pleasure rooted in the non-closure of a gazing-commons aesthetic, with its yearning for otherness in the non-appropriative mode? By not ignoring the differences between the personal and the political, but on the contrary, by showing how these differences resonate together in unpredictable and contingent ways to form, in the words of Gilles Deleuze:[23] *planes of consistency* from which new political concepts can be formed.

So what does the brand *contemporary art* presently suggest for a gazing-common aesthetic? Not much, yet. Julian Stallabrass argues[24] that behind contemporary art's multiplicity and apparent capriciousness lies a monstrous, bleak uniformity and that this amounts to making culture uncurious, timid, and stupid in the service of a big business ethos of unquestioning consumer conformity. Also, Stallabrass purports that the unregulated insular contemporary art market seeks to dupe newbie art rubes into being enthusiastic participants in the dumbing-down values useful to big business; values which address all communications to the lowest common denominator of the monstrously massive. So, the obvious question is: what about art's responsibility of resistance? Perhaps surprisingly, for me, the answer is to be found within the challenge of a noise style based in resistance through the cultivation of invisibility.[25] So I want to argue for *vOluptuary drOid décOlletage* an agony of style of

[22] As I have done with my own work while also collecting examples of many other artist's work that can be placed in this continuum.

[23] Gilles Deleuze conceived of philosophy as the production of concepts, and he characterized himself as a "pure metaphysician." In his magnum opus *Difference and Repetition*, he tries to develop a metaphysics adequate to contemporary mathematics and science—a metaphysics in which the concept of multiplicity replaces that of substance, event replaces essence, and virtuality replaces possibility. Deleuze also produced studies in the history of philosophy (on Hume, Nietzsche, Kant, Bergson, Spinoza, Foucault, and Leibniz) and on the arts (a two-volume study of the cinema, books on Proust and Sacher-Masoch, a work on the painter Francis Bacon, and a collection of essays on literature). Deleuze considered these latter works as pure philosophy, and not criticism, since he sought to create the concepts that correspond to the artistic practices of painters, filmmakers, and writers. In 1968, he met Félix Guattari, a political activist and radical psychoanalyst, with whom he wrote several works, among them the two-volume *Capitalism and Schizophrenia*, comprised of *Anti-Oedipus* (1972) and *A Thousand Plateaus* (1980). Their final collaboration was *What Is Philosophy?* (1991).

[24] See Stallabrass (2006).

[25] Perhaps this should not be surprising given the hidden complexity of a basic Internet transaction is a mystery to most users: Sending a message with photographs to a neighbor could involve a trip

logo invisibility—and the importance that should be given to noise art aesthetic struggles for a gazing-commons.

The principle of constructing patterns of infinite becomings is perhaps inherent in avant-garde artistic tradition (avant-garde values). Graham Harman suggested as much. But this avant-garde now, I think, should be considered in terms of noisy invisibility not ontology, as deviating from the regularities of visible normality provides the avant-garde new sources for artistic production. Certainly, the values of the avant-garde have always been interfering with the channels of artistic production and reception—and these values are responsible for expanding the forms and definitions of art itself.[26] But like in nature, noise in art plays a productive role in the invisible life of a system when it stresses becoming-imperceptible.

But a becoming-imperceptible-invisible monster sacré, today can no longer be a form of enfant terrible with-drawl, akin to Marcel Duchamp's strategic invisibility,[27] but rather a phantasmagorical plunge into what Félix Guattari expresses as the *chaosmosis*.[28] In that sense, *vOluptuary drOid décOlletage* marks a qualitative transformation into a non-place where being and non-being reverse into each other, unfolding out and enfolding in their respective outsides. This short-circuit causes a creative conflagration typical of the art of noise.

Let's consider the difference between noise art (based on an individual's inner vision) and the monstrous mass machine data market,[29] with its digital functionalism. For me the difference is in looking *into* and projecting *onto* something—thereby discovering an emerging manifestation based in invisibility—as opposed to looking *at* something. In that sense it requires an active slow participation on the part of the viewer—and noise style demands as much. For me this requires use of hidden mental participation and, as such, is now essential in our climate of monstrous mass media (mass-think) in that it plays against the grain of given objective consensus visibility.

However, my main interest in *vOluptuary drOid décOlletage* as invisibility lay in a texture of emerging claims of art-as-politics, with its emphasis on the production

---

through hundreds or thousands of miles of Internet conduits and multiple data centers before the e-mail arrives across the street.

[26] For more on this read my essay "Viractuality in the Webbed Digital Age" that was published in *M/E/A/N/I/N/G* Online #5 25th Anniversary Edition (2011). http://writing.upenn.edu/pepc/meaning/05/meaning-online-5.html#nechvatal

[27] Duchamp's entire artistic activity since the "definitive incompletion" of the *Large Glass* in 1923 was an exercise in strategic invisibility, giving rise to objects and events which—because they were apparently too impermanent or unimportant or insubstantial, or because they eluded established genre conventions, or because they confused or diluted authorial identity—evaded recognition as "works of art."

[28] Félix Guattari said in his noteworthy book, *Chaosmosis: An Ethico-Aesthetic Paradigm*, the work of art, for those who use it, is an activity of unframing, of rupturing sense, of baroque proliferation or extreme impoverishment that leads to a recreation and a reinvention of the subject itself.

[29] To support all that digital activity, there are now more than 3 million data centers of widely varying sizes worldwide, according to figures from the International Data Corporation.

of individuality based in a political physiology (a political function of living systems) with a strong proposition of emergence as the key aspect.

II

Noise nourishes a new order.
—Michele Serres, *The Parasite*

Now I would like to look more specifically at the possibility of further developments in noise art aesthetics concerning where becoming-imperceptible and becoming-perceptible nimbly interact. As sketched out in my book *Immersion Into Noise*, the evolution of visual noise art develops from certain pre-historic cave areas and baroque grottoes, to certain levels of mannerist and counter-mannerist complexity, to noisy spatial renderings in various exuberant architectural styles, then into cubism, futurism, dada, fluxus, and other twentieth-century avant-garde movements, into the screech of technological noise art, and into the softness of software noise art aesthetics.

As noted above, what is important in the art of noise aesthetics is its intentional and elongated invisibility[30] and enigma. That is why this subject is so hard to write about. The very topic is a very difficult one to pin down and make intelligible for good reason. The art of noise is an art of disbelief in habitual codes of practice and understanding. You must take the art of noise on its own terms or risk doing violence to the art.

Noise art is not a set of homogeneous practices but a complex field converging around perceived weaknesses in the art system. Such a noisy hyper-cognitive stance happens when the particular of electronic connectivity is seen as part of an accrual total system by virtue of its being connected to everything else—while remaining dissonant. Noise aesthetics is a complex and ambiguous political gazing, and its theory of an art of resistance and investigation would be increasingly valuable to an analytical social movement based on skepticism while undermining monstrous market predictabilities, as it strengthens unique personal powers of imagination and critical thinking. This is so as it counters the effects of our age of simplification: effects which have resulted from the glut of consumer-oriented entertainment messages and political propaganda which the monstrous mass media feeds us daily in the interests of corporate profit and governmental psychological manipulations.

The noise art aesthetic behind *vOluptuary drOid décOlletage* is one of dissonant immersion into a maelstrom of glossolaliaic unintelligibility, chaos, and exaltation.

[30] This parallels the fact that in many data facilities, servers are loaded with applications and left to run indefinitely, even after nearly all users have vanished or new versions of the same programs are running elsewhere. At a certain point, no one is responsible anymore, because no one, absolutely no one, wants to go in that room and unplug a server.

Its style function is a way of seeing that reverses the order of figure/ground[31] to ground/figure. *vOluptuary drOid décOlletage* collapses being into a state of non-being ontological implosion. It creates ambivalent aleatory[32] processes that are true to our inner essential world: dynamic pools of expansion and disintegration.

The art of noise is that screech amid the collapse and extension of aesthetics connected to immanence and transcendence (where art is in the process of becoming-imperceptible-perceptible) facing the merging of figure into environment and environment into figure. We can find moments of this screech of collapse-extension in contemporary complexity theory and in some areas of information technology, nano-technology, cognitive science, and biotechnology. These moments of collapse-extension accompany the contemporary development where the static image has become dynamically engaged with the human imagination and personal choices of the viewer. In some cases, literally, engaging the participation of the viewer (who becomes what I have elsewhere renamed as the *viewpant*) (Nechvatal 2009) to the point of physical interactivity. In other cases they are engaged conceptually (or post-conceptually) by looking long and hard at the art.

Noise art aesthetics prefers the becoming-imperceptible invisibility of the latter, as the participants in this eye-catching trend absorb into the work without engaging in the process of exposing their actions of external choices and events to measure and objectification (to some extent), and thus to the participation of the public in more or less advanced forms of control and reification. I believe that the forms of this aesthetic post-conceptual participation can be a decisive element in offering generative possibilities of development that will continue to be interesting and supportive of the gazing-commons.

The unwanted becoming-perceptible trend is likewise evident if we consider another aspect: the spread through social media technologies of content that uses visualization and data monitoring, for example, systems that survey and process in real-time preferences and movements of viewpants via mobile networks. The same becoming-perceptible tendency holds for many net-art projects. So process-based data monitoring design and algorithmic architecture have now passed through the experimental phase and begun to have anti-commons practical uses. What we have witnessed for art through this development, coupled with relational art aesthetics, is on the one hand a spilling over toward entertainment and, on the other, a growing integration with fast data monitoring surveillance.

In defense of the individual-based commons, my theory of the aesthetics of an art of noise encourages data monitoring *deferral*. Seen as too *difficult* by some, for me the paucity of clean art at a fast glance conceals the riches of associational gazing with respect to the combinatory dynamics of leisurely layered creations.

---

[31] The characteristic organization of perception into a figure that "stands out" against an undifferentiated background, e.g., a printed word against a background page. What is figural at any one moment depends on patterns of sensory stimulation and on the momentary interests of the perceiver.

[32] Aleatoricism is the incorporation of chance into the process of creation, especially the creation of art or media. The word derives from the Latin word *alea*, the rolling of dice.

In that regard, consider the large quantities of subtle kinds of noise that have proliferated since electricity, especially so since the onset of information revolution at the end of the 1970s. With it came a low-impact noise emitted by every kind of electrical appliance, contributing to the white-noise dense texture of our acoustic environment.[33] Such a post-industrial white noise environment is ambiguously omnipresent and mostly subliminal.

My suggestion for art noise aesthetics is, I believe, fully able to render sensible the white noise sequencing when it uses subliminal latent excess in its presentational mode, and when avoiding over-determination like the plague. Because such an excess overload of representation offers us a measure of freedom of choice in how we unpack it (or not). The greater amount of stimulation-information needed,[34] the greater the uncertainty that the "message" (proposition) offers. That is why my preference has been for semi-abstract, palimpsest-like work, like *vOluptuary drOid décOlletage*, that contains subliminal latent excess. It has greater freedom of choice, and greater uncertainty, due to an excess of information via the ground/figure catastrophic collapse. This is what it takes to make nimble art, if we consider that clean pop is that which the art of noise defines itself against. Pop spectacle is the outside of noise cultural aesthetics at large.

My concern here is with the ethical and liberating use of representation (and anti-representation) within the broader image environment. By attempting to represent the monster sacrés aesthetic as non-representable (as the hugeness of post-industrial white noise is ubiquitously if subtlety present) one can obliterate the proper object of re-representation through the awareness/consciousness of gazing aesthetic bursts. This stress on the alterity and ineffability of noise that eludes our fuzzy grasp of its grandeur is what *hyper-noise* art is about.

The term *hyper-noise* is my theory of noise art as constructed via connected-competing vectors and figure/grounds (Nechvatal 2011, p. 3[illegible]). This concept owes something to Quentin Meillassoux's idea of *hyper-Chaos* that was sketched out in his book *After Finitude*: a form of absolutization where nothing is impossible or unthinkable (Meillassoux 2008). It must be grasped that hyper-Chaos is not just disorder but that it also may produce order and stability, even little static worlds, as well as complete destruction of what is.

Hyper-noise art refuses easy consumption and encourages love, because a love for noise art will make perturbing events in your life more tolerable. It will make you able to see and hear more and make you more adaptable to disturbance, rather than being torn up about them. It will help you to avoid psychic ossification by your loving latent expanse. This is what suggests referring hyper-noise art to the aesthetics of the *sublime*, which, in the eighteenth century, was linked to the grandness of natural phenomena. Now hyper-noise art is an innovative version of the sublime in which, for the first time, the embeddedness that we recognize ourselves in

[33] For more on this see Schafer (1994).

[34] The New York Stock Exchange produces up to 2000 GB of data per day that must be stored for years.

(concerning white noise) matches up with our subliminal inner noise world. This embedded awareness can be produced by noisy artistic becomings.

Generative hyper-noise art is perhaps the most evident example of this hyper-noise sublime opportunity, as post-conceptual generative art serves to produce unpredictable results, both when it is based on arithmetic instructions contained in code and in other ritual rules. So hyper-noise software art means primarily some form of generative or semi-generative art, in which the artist establishes the operational tenets/choices that are calculated to act autonomously or semi-autonomously.

The above-mentioned white-hyper-noise dense texture of our acoustic environment, with its uniformity and lack of variance, suggests to me a possibility of connecting ourselves psychically to the great chain of being (that which proceeds us and of which we are apart) through contemporary art. However, this requires an active imagination that is aided by the visualization properties offered up in the art of noise.

This potential of noise art aesthetics is embedded in the recognition of our sheer potentiality: all the selves we have within to develop or burn out. All the worlds we might create or destroy. Hyper-noise art shows us that we are more diverse than we had imagined, and more tolerant. It points out that what we have in common is a dangerous propensity for overrating our powers of comprehension.

But noise art aesthetics is hostile to generalizations. It is recalcitrant by design. It affirms with jubilation our state of varied mutability. That is my general standard of excellence for it.

Noise art aesthetics behind *vOluptuary drOid décOlletage* tears our phallogocentricism apart to confront the diversity in us, and in each other. This lesson is a necessity, and the recognition of this necessity is part of the peculiar pleasure that noise art affords us. A pleasure clearly of rapturous abandonment where the intended effect is an inner liberation by means of de-simulation. Noise art aesthetics opens up in us a sense of possibility that we understand and feel at one and the same time to be both dangerous and indispensable. It points us toward the perilous turbulences and chancy exhilarations that pass through us: overcast, heartbroken, eloquent passages that pull us apart even as they discharge pent-up repressed ways of accepted common wisdom. So, my initiative for a hyper-noise art aesthetic is not a swoon to an intricate inner violence. Rather, it more has the look of analogon.[35]

vOluptuary drOid décOlletage is a return to the shifting ground on which art rests. It gives us a sense of discovery that marked art's beginning. It is an alternative, phantasmagorical way to express the agitation between form and the ground. *vOluptuary drOid décOlletage* is beautiful negativity.

Its incomprehensibility by design connects the commons to our unconscious mind and inner feelings through what I think to be a type of chaos magic.[36] Through

[35] Analogue: something that bears an analogy to something else.

[36] Some common sources of inspiration for chaos magic include such diverse areas as science fiction, scientific theories, ceremonial magic, shamanism, Eastern philosophy, and individual experimentation.

a variety of techniques often reminiscent of Western ceremonial magic or indigenous shamanism, many practitioners of chaos magic believe they can change both their subjective experience and objective reality. Although there are a few techniques unique to chaos magic (such as some forms of sigil magic), chaos magic is often highly individualistic and borrows liberally from other belief systems. In this way, some chaos magicians consider their practice to be a meta-belief. But I consider it to be a phantasmagoric art of noise.

Chaoist noise art creates the visualization bridge between form and intuition, as its uncertain images have more information in them than a clear certain image (or sound) where the information quickly becomes redundant. Thus noise art aesthetics gives rise to new thought. It promotes the emergence of new forms of an old story: art.

As mentioned above, what is important in *vOluptuary drOid décOlletage* is its intentional enigma. It needs to be obscure to the degree that its codes cannot be discerned. This phantasmagorical obscurity and mystery is increasingly desirable in a world that has become increasingly data-mined, mapped, quantified, specialized, and identified in a straightforward matter of fact way. This will for enigma is the basis for discovering and entering into an immersion into the art of noise, even.[37]

Such aesthetic enigma is alluring when intelligible mining-type data processing is perceived as hollow, trite, and insensitive. Its goal is to disrupt instrumental logic and contradict, counteract, and cancel out false reason and hollow feeling.

What also is behind the *vOluptuary drOid décOlletage* aesthetic is the extent to which it urges the mind toward transformations. Here art is the infinite space of hyper-chaos[38] imagination. The hyper-chaos art noise dynamic exceeds the art world to the point where this dynamic empowers art to oppose that which threatens it (money)—as the strategy of a dissonant hyper-anything (Nechvatal 2011, p. 32) includes principles of networked connections and electronic links that give multiple choices of passages to follow and continually new branching possibilities. Instead of stressing the reflective limits imposed by the category of art—the art of noise aesthetic can attempt to specify the resistance embodied within it. So noise art's counter to the spectacle's misery consists in not forgetting or denying spectacle but in an interruption of it with a phantasmagorical semi-remembering of pre-spectacular suffering through which human grief is at one and the same time relived and relieved. Suffering and joy, like figure and ground, are here tied together, neither one without the other. Constantly flickering. Thus *vOluptuary drOid décOlletage* aesthetics suggests and produces stress in us; one might even say an urgent anxiety of disintegration. So dedication to its merits, if there are any, might well be described

---

[37] As an example, see/hear Marina Rosenfeld's *Cephissus landscape* (2002), an immersive noise work that undermines the central notion of "surround-sound" technology by locating viewers in an environment with no fixed center and numerous temporary sonic sweet spots where short bursts of mingled electronic and acoustic sounds intersect and decay in expanding concentric circles that suggest oscillate landscapes.

[38] See Quentin Meillassoux's idea of *hyper-Chaos* in his compelling book *After Finitude* where it is defined as a form of *absolutization where nothing is impossible or unthinkable* (Meillassoux 2008).

as vaguely heroic, because noise art aesthetics suggests the revelation of a plentiful nihilistic life force. Thus noise art aesthetics can be as creative as it is destructive. Or implies an endless struggle between the two. In that sense it is a cul-de-sac of ill communication (vacuole)[39]—the communication of enigma itself.

So *vOluptuary drOid décOlletage* has something about it that words risk diminishing. Nevertheless, I obviously have felt that I must take that risk because if we are to continue to live among electronic vibrations that mine us, it may be helpful to talk back against them. But yes, *vOluptuary drOid décOlletage* is a transmitter of unspeakable secrets that want *more* from us. Moreover, it invites us *to want more from art*. It asks us to look *deeper*.

There are now many artists who see the symbolic and metaphorical dimension of a work as of little importance. I am not one of them. For me, the real worth of vigorous contemporary art is in its ability to deliver to the commons excessive sensually embodied implications. As noise art aesthetics are indistinguishable from that which it produces as the art of noise, it might be considered as a panpsychic[40] sphere that contains systems of chance operations within it. What more can we ask of this hectic art of noise aesthetics, that *vOluptuary drOid décOlletage* manifests, than making art again unpredictably alive enough to produce palimpsest vision.

Biographical Note

Joseph Nechvatal's digital paintings, such as *vOluptuary drOid décOlletage*, conjure up an enigmatic world of almost dreadful depth—a depth that signals the dynamic critical intricacy of a contemporary practice engaged in the fragile wedding of image production and image resistance. His computer-robotic-assisted paintings and animations are made up of an oddly excessive concoction of ambiguous sexual body parts (morphed from both sexes) and expressions of political ire that address the global influence of the viral form. Nechvatal brings a subversive reading to computational media by presenting an artistic consciousness that articulates contemporary concerns regarding safety, truth, identity, and objectivity.

Since 1986 Joseph Nechvatal has worked with ubiquitous electronic visual information, computers, and computer-robotics. His computer-robotic-assisted paintings and computer software animations are shown regularly in galleries and museums throughout the world. From 1991 to 1993 he worked as artist-in-resident at the Louis Pasteur Atelier and the Saline Royale/Ledoux Foundation's computer lab in

[39] This is a reference to Gilles Deleuze's (1925–1995) notion of the vacuole. This concept of non-communication comes from Deleuze's *Postscript on Control Societies*. Deleuze's notion of control is connected to information-communication technology—a concept he pulled out of the work of William S. Burroughs (1914–1997). A vacuole is like a sac in a cell's membrane, completely bound up inside the cell but also separate from it. Vacuoles play a significant role in autophagy, maintaining an *imbalance* between biogenesis (production) and *degradation* (or turnover) of many substances and cell structures. They also aid in the destruction of invading bacteria or of misfolded proteins that have begun to build up within the cell. The vacuole is a major part of the plant and animal cell (Nechvatal 2011, p. 14).

[40] Panpsychism is the view that all matter has a mental aspect, or, alternatively, all objects have a unified center of experience or point of view.

Arbois, France, on *The Computer Virus Project*: an experiment with computer viruses as a creative stratagem. In 2002 he extended that artistic research into the field of viral artificial life through his collaboration with the programmer Stéphane Sikora.

Nechvatal earned his PhD in the philosophy of art and new technology at the Centre for Advanced Inquiry in the Interactive Arts (CAiiA), University of Wales College, Newport, UK. From 1999 to 2013, Nechvatal taught at the School of Visual Arts in New York City (SVA). His book of essays *Towards an Immersive Intelligence: Essays on the Work of Art in the Age of Computer Technology and Virtual Reality (1993–2006)* was published by Edgewise Press in 2009. In 2011 his book *Immersion Into Noise* was published by the University of Michigan Library's Scholarly Publishing Office in conjunction with the Open Humanities Press.

References

James Bamford, *The Shadow Factory: The Ultra-Secret NSA from 9/11 to the Eavesdropping on America*. Anchor (2009).

Claire Bishop, "Antagonism and Relational Aesthetics" *October* (Fall 2004, No. 110), p. 52.

Simon Critchley, "Absolutely-Too-Much", *Brooklyn Rail*, Summer issue 2012. http://www.brooklynrail.org/2012/08/art/absolutely-too-much

Manuel DeLanda, *New Materialism: Interviews & Cartographies by Rick Dolphijn and Iris van der Tuin*, Ann Arbor: Open Humanities Press (2012) p. 38.

Gilles Deleuze, Félix Guattari, *A Thousand Plateaus. Capitalism and Schizophrenia*, translation by Brian Massumi, University of Minnesota Press (1987) p. 279.

Chad Hensley, "The Beauty of Noise: An Interview with Masami Akita of Merzbow" in Cox, Cristoph & Warner, Daniel (ed.): *Audio Culture: Readings in Modern Music*. New York: Continuum (2004).

Quentin Meillassoux, *After Finitude: An Essay on the Necessity of Contingency*, trans. Ray Brassier, London: Continuum (2008), p. 64.

Joseph Nechvatal, *Immersive Ideals/Critical Distances*, LAP Lambert Academic Publishing (2009), p. 56.

Joseph Nechvatal, *Immersion Into Noise*. Ann Arbor: Open Humanities Press (2011).

R. Murray Schafer, *The Soundscape: Our Sonic Environment and the Tuning of the World*, Destiny Books (1994).

Julian Stallabrass, *Contemporary Art: A Very Short Introduction*, Oxford University Press (2006).

Natural Challenges "Extension on One Chord", Venice Biennale 2015: Notes of a Participating Artist

Fré Ilgen

Fré Ilgen, *Extension on One Chord.* Sculpture, 2007. Stainless steel, wood, paint. H228 x W166,1 x D59,1 cm (H89.75 x W65.4 x D23.25"). FRONTIERS REIMAGINED – Art that Connects Us, Tagore Foundation International, Palazzo Grimani, 2015, Venice, Italy

F. Ilgen (✉)
Berlin, Germany

F. Franco (ed.), *Computational Art at the Venice Biennale (1970–2015)*, Springer Series on Cultural Computing, https://doi.org/10.1007/978-3-032-04258-3_5

Introduction

As artist my personal main focus is not on digital art but on the so-called traditional media, though I always have had a profound interest in technology. As long ago as 1996, I was privileged to experience Virtual Reality as an artist in residency at LUTCHI-Loughborough University, in those important years under the visionary leadership of Professor Ernest Edmonds, the important English pioneer of digital art. An immediate experience with high-tech that took its time but made its mark on my own work. Besides, I have regularly been involved in art and science encounters, in the past 10 years, specifically on art and neuroscience.

As theorist and writer my main concern is figuring out *what* works of art can offer any other person, not so much distinguishing between kinds of art, or if a work of art would question anything or what socio-political message would be expressed. Why do we all agree art is communication, information, and interaction, but we do not actually study how this works and what consequences for art itself we can learn by studying the actual interaction of the viewer with the viewed in normal circumstances? For whom do we make our art: for our peers, for curators, or for the art-loving public? Especially as we can easily admit the audience in the art world is not exactly uninformed or uneducated. Questions that are certainly also applicable to digital arts in all forms and variations.

Art and the Viewer in General

In digital arts there are quite a few artists who merely seek approval from or have business interest in the industries. A given that comes natural with the technology provided by the same industries. I prefer addressing the genuinely creative artists. It has always been and still is the natural attitude of the artist to follow the inner drive, hence to first and foremost follow the ego, but also it certainly should come natural and is inevitable for artists to keep the viewer, the other, in mind. Being allowed to contribute to another person's individual experience, maybe even to another person's life, is the only actual and factual social-political meaning of an artwork.

Regardless of the endless attempts since the late 1960s to prove the mind, the intellectualisation, the verbalised statement, to be most important, the first and foremost encounter of any viewer with an artefact is predominantly visual and the most basic natural process of interaction of the human with his/her immediate environment. This undoubtedly should matter also to digital art in any form, and, as neuroscience demonstrates, does not merely involve the eye-thalamus-visual cortex, but involves the whole body and hence the whole natural behaviour of the exhibition visitor.

Technology as Technology: Supporting Creativity

In the studio in traditional media, the choices, kinds, and qualities of oil or acrylic paints, crayons, canvas, paper, or plaster, clay, wood or steel, and the tools play decisive roles in immediate interaction with the sizes of the given space, the quality of light, and fresh air and are of inevitable influence. Outside the studio a whole other experiential and perceptual ballgame evolves. The artist who has done many exhibitions, who is also interested in, aware of, and probably sensitive to the viewer's responses, will take such experiences and observations back to the studio.

As such it can be posed that any artistic medium, and the application of any technology, might work for certain purposes, for example, enhancing an artist's creativity (my own experience with VR), like any traditional tool helps making a specific work, but does not work by itself when displayed in natural given exhibition situations. Early examples are how photography importantly triggered inspiration in artists, for instance, Eugene Delacroix, or Auguste Rodin, while in the end they focused on the artwork being made in the so-called traditional media. Later in his life, Delacroix used photographs of models as starting point for a new painting, while during the painting process the whole form and composition would change. This is a process of natural transformation and not merely photo-realism. Rodin often commissioned creative photographers, whose photos provided him with inspiration for new sculptural experiments.

Distinguishing between photography as art form and photography and video as recording technologies, the last may support and inspire an artist in the studio. I experience since many years that both photography and video recordings provide me with a fresh look on the evolving artwork, comparable to how it can be helpful to occasionally look through a mirror at a painting or sculpture one is making, or look at the work in an upside-down position.

Notes on Visitors at a Biennale

When a viewer encounters an artwork in an exhibition, most features that matter to the artist in his studio hardly play a role anymore, but a complexity of other factors do. For a large part visitors to biennales (and museums) are focused on personal enjoyment of the whole event, meaning they focus and plan on seeing as much as they can absorb on a particular day. The experiencing and learning process factually diverts their personal focus away from their own daily concerns.

In plain words: the art should provide a general sense of meaningful fun and pleasure but should also offer sufficient surprise and natural perceptual appeal to be able to potentially offer the brain of the viewer causes for diverting this focus. Along such lines one may quickly conclude that artworks are experienced by art viewers as having substantial meaning when the right amount of complex visual incentives is provided. Visual incentives of the artwork that naturally persuade the viewer to linger and look long enough at that same artwork. The repetition of the eyes roaming the work causes the brain paths involved in processing this visual activity to lead to a diversion of the main attention (in most people their normal everyday concerns about business, job, family, politics, taxes, health), thus will have an experience the involved person may define as "meaningful". Befitting the particular circumstances of the exhibition, and as such accommodating the viewer wishing to experience the whole event, the artwork should offer all this in a relatively short time. Needless to add that the best artworks offer enough that a viewer may find even more visually appealing factors, causing him/her to look longer. The opposite is offered by too minimal and too perfectly made artworks.

Viewers strolling around often unconsciously and instantaneously decide to look at something just quickly or a bit longer. For obvious reasons this is a natural behaviour and is entirely opposed to all intellectualised statements provided for every single artwork presented at biennales, and in museums. Such statements are good for providing those who upon the first encounter wish to know what the artist's intentions are but factually are only for accommodating the curators, art press, and other art professionals. At events like biennales one certainly may question if the artists would be aware for whom they make and present their work: for the public, for the other, or regarding career options aiming only at museums and art press?

My Own Participation at the 2015 Biennale Venice

Yes, I plead guilty, as artist I am depending on career options myself, thus on what my peers and other art professionals decide, but certainly like to think my artworks may contribute to other person's individual and personal lives, maybe even offer them experiences that help them cope with their own lives.

Thanks to my generous gallerist my large work "Extension on One Chord" is included in the exhibition "Frontiers Reimagined" at the Museo di Palazzo Grimani, formal part of the Biennale Collaterale Program in Venice. This exhibition, curated by Sundaram Tagore (New York, Hong Kong, Singapore) in collaboration with the acknowledged English art historian Marius Kwint, contains works of quite a few artists from actually all around the world, presented at equal level. All quite accomplished artists whom I am proud to be shown with.

My work, a large wall sculpture in stainless steel and wood, is coloured and effectively displayed on a long and bluish-grey painted wall. The work itself may be formally described as abstract and simulating a complexity of centrifugal and centripetal motions, clearly preannouncing all the work I do today. The sense of nongravity the work allows in principle can be led back to my experience with virtual reality at Loughborough University, while the specific colour application—fragmented and spread in a certain sequence over the work—quite likely can be retraced to my fascination for the American artist and friend Charles Biederman (1906–2004). Maybe even the Baroque swirls of interlacing motions, though Charles would not exactly have agreed this feature of his own work to be defined as Baroque.

In this particular work from 2007, the title referring to a great song of Ten Years After (sorry, I am from that generation), I explored the perceptual power between stainless steel as industrially perfect material with the roughness of a natural wooden shape, in principle exemplifying the theme of Eros and Thanatos of my recent works. Later I understood this contrast to work so fine because for specific natural reasons humans prefer looking at works that are not perfectly made, but show natural marks like marks made by human hands. In art history, though often meant differently, this is the notion of the unfinished.

My furthered understanding of visual perception, backed up by many observations I made of art viewers all over the world, in museums, galleries, in private collections, but also in cathedrals and temples, and learning especially by frequent encounters with neuroscientists, certainly including leading US neuroscientist Dr Partha Mitra (Mitra-Lab, CSHL, NY), have led me personally to conclude that perceptually there is not so much difference between figuration and abstraction. Through natural alignment processes in one's brain figurative elements in artworks appeal more naturally and immediately. Thus my work has progressively become more figurative in painting as well as in sculpture, while the simulated motions are still decisively present like in works like "Extension on One Chord".

Natural Challenges (for Digital Art)

There certainly is some good digital art around. I happen to enjoy the continuous development of Manfred Mohr, who keeps coming up with new surprising steps. I probably like his works because Manfred creates works that size-wise and kind-like are close matches to how many viewers like viewing and experiencing artworks in their personal home situations either as paintings or as small screens.

Importantly, digital art should mainly be based on perception, while too often it still is merely technically savvy. This means, digital art can only be considered a separate art form and labelled as such when it does not merely attempt to copy what has been done in other media all the time, like simulating painting or making movies. Besides, based on perceptual values as mentioned, one has to consider the following questions.

It is remarkable to note that at this year's biennale hardly any digital art is presented. Can one exhibit digital artworks just anywhere, expecting the work will find a natural appeal in the viewer, whose focus is seeing not this particular artwork alone, but seeing the whole museum or biennale? While traditional artworks, paintings and sculptures (I am not talking about torn car tires), allow any viewer in a split second to decide for themselves if they like to look at the work at all or not, how can digital art allow the viewer the same degree of free choice? Obviously I do not mean the kinds of digital art that in principle mimic traditional media. What does this imply for the darkened room? When a person goes to a cinema his/her attention is focused on sitting in a darkened space watching one movie, a well-proven concept. Now try forcing such persons check out five movies in separate spaces.

From the angle of the viewer, can the perfection of digitally made artworks (both two- and three-dimensional), that are inevitably perfect because of the technical processing, compete with the natural higher appeal of imperfection in traditional media?

Internationally one still sees art projections on large screens or whole walls in darkened spaces for which the creativity of the presented work seems to matter much less than the awesome display of the latest in hardware and software capacities. Is this a smart wink to or from the high-tech and movie industries? The display at the Korean pavilion, for instance, consists of several wall-covering monitors, displaying some imaginary short SF story. One cannot help but question if such a techno-impressive overkill would not just as well work when displaying a soccer game. The awesome technological presentation does the work, like any consumer electronics fair or shop showing the latest, the biggest, the most sensational, not what is actually shown, but is a museum or the biennale the proper place?

While acknowledging the reasoning of energy companies and high-tech companies that all art should be made depending on their products, this tendency has made the gap much wider between the art presented and the art desired by a larger audience. Like one can clearly observe in the global art market, artists are gradually becoming aware that for their own survival they need to consider the viewer as possible and only real target group.

In all art fairs, also at the Venice Biennale, one may observe a tendency looping back to traditional media, supported by a conservative choice of galleries and curators as well as by the attention of the visitors. In Venice, I learned that quite a few visitors did not like going into the dark rooms with videos, were appalled by the blaring video monitors, nor liked looking at the various electricity-driven devices, but adored and profoundly enjoyed the "Collaterale" exhibitions with paintings and sculptures.

Could it be that the focus of attention as pure basic feature of how humans naturally function and behave, of which quite a part can be traced back to the basic processes of our biological organism (mind/body as whole), naturally makes traditional media to just work better, while digital media work at specific moments, at specific sites, for specific purposes, for a specific audience?

This may sound provocative, maybe reactionary to some, possibly blasphemous, but is simply based on the humanness of humans. At least in the past 50–60 years in the art world all professionals have passionately been involved in emphasising their messages, statements, meanings, questioning, rattling, imprinting innovation, while in fact steadily, quasi systematically, entirely forgetting, ignoring, or downright disregarding the viewer.

The final truth about any exhibition is not the quantity of visitors clicked by a museum guard but the time visitors as an average spend in front of individual artworks. Innovation in art is a misleading directive because the basic perimeters of the viewer's mind/body have not evolved much in a few millennia.

Biographical Note

Fré Ilgen, Dutch artist, theorist, lives and works in Berlin, Germany.

Author of three major books:

"ART? No Thing! *Analogies between art, science and philosophy*", Pro Foundation /Artists Bookworks, 2004.

"ARTIST? *The Hypothesis of Bodiness*", Wasmuth Verlag, 2014.

"The viewer? *The Actual Purpose of Art*", Studio Ilgen, 2022.

Orly Aviv: "Nervous Organ", Venice 2015

Maureen Kendal

This digital interactive art installation was shown in the European Cultural Centre, Palazzo Bembo and Palazzo Mora, a local gallery near to the official Venice Biennale. http://www.palazzomora.org

Over the summer of 2015 in Venice, at least 1000 people a day explored Orly Aviv's "Nervous Organ". Aviv's artistic journey was an adventure into time, space, and existence. Opening up into an imaginative trajectory, "Nervous Organ" took the participatory audience far beyond the eye of the beholder. Aviv's background in computer and Informatics Science enables translation from her imagination into a virtual and immersive submergence simulation of dancing "under the sea". The work was shown in Venice, Palazzo Mora, from May to November 2015.

https://www.youtube.com/watch?v=eJ5ftyoX4H0

Aviv's habitual domain is the seascape and the sandy shoreline. From her early childhood and as a digital artist today, her home is close to the sea, on the beach. As a postgraduate student in London at the Slade School of Art, she yearned for the sea, but traveling down on a cold autumnal October to Brighton, she discovered that the English Channel offered only a harsh, cold, stony beach and pier, far removed from the white gentle sand beaches of her life in Israel. Unable to swim in the grey chilly sea, she explored Brighton's historical Aquarium. Early video tests led to advanced technical experiments to capture quality footage that sought to simulate an immersive diving experience.

Through her artistic practice, Aviv expansively shares her sensorial experiences of aquatic immersion. "Nervous Organ" as an aquatic sensual experience offers a therapeutic encounter where the inner emotional world can be synthesised with external experience. Offering a sense of safety, an opportunity to forget external

M. Kendal (✉)
London, United Kingdom
e-mail: maureen@dreamstudio.io

F. Franco (ed.), *Computational Art at the Venice Biennale (1970–2015)*, Springer Series on Cultural Computing, https://doi.org/10.1007/978-3-032-04258-3_6

realities, and be immersed cinematically in an aesthetic, simulated Under the Sea experience.

"Nervous Organ" simulates deep sea diving in a wired semi-dark room. The sophisticated software, which was designed specifically for this project, controls all of the systems smooth. The visitors can trigger pressure sensors, which activate full wall video projections and music. The visitors become participants as they navigate through the room and decide where and when to see the video or hear the music. The sensual harmonic music is composed from ocean and forest sounds, evoking the calls of whales and dolphins. The video footage shows diverse and colourful marine environments.

"Nervous Organ" shows diverse marine animals, from the tiny orange dragon through the blue jellyfish dancers to the huge sharks and whales. Orly explained, "*I feel all the ocean creatures are equal, they all need each other to survive and fertilise, it is one ecosystem, we have the responsibility to keep them all live*". Orly Aviv hoped that through playing, dancing, and enjoying the "Nervous Organ" room visitors could create a strong positive bond to the ocean. Appreciation of kinaesthetic pleasure evoked within the "Nervous Organ" encourages socio-ecological initiatives that protect the ocean to keep it alive for future generations.

Aviv's artistic practice evokes her concern with enriching personal response and relationships; thinking beyond "the self", not only in terms of external realities but also from within oneself. While appreciating sociopolitical challenges of our time, Aviv is working within a different perspective, by deepening our hearts, minds, and bodies, to feel beyond, focusing on connecting the inner with the external.

Aviv's vision is: "*To create the relationship between the artist and audience, where the audience can flow with their thoughts, I want to open up an associative field, for the person to be embraced and open up his/her imagination from which associative emotions can emerge*". The process of immersive engagement offers a return to a memory and the emergence of a new or imagined feeling that is quite different and distinct from the artist's original inspiration. During her artistic practice, Aviv has been investigating ways to communicate this sense of new radical vision through the enabling of an emerging capability of her audience.

Aviv is a polymath, working across interdisciplinary areas. She explains how her art practice is linked to her scientific investigations: "*When people observe my artwork, I am focussed on their automatic reaction: Their body language, their eye movements, emotions, the brief seconds of 'remembering' 'knowing' 'familiarity'. I am concerned with the very existence of the inner process of this phenomenon. I have a raw feeling, that there is a key that stimulates, generates what first looks as a sporadic colourful visual 'mind bubbles'. For the last few years I am carrying out research in the lab of Professor Moshe Bar, a neuroscientist, director of the Gonda Multidisciplinary Brain Research Centre at Bar-Ilan University, Israel, searching for that KEY*".

At the Global Arts Foundation at the Palazzo Mora, during the Venice Biennale, Aviv's "Nervous Organ" shimmered significantly. The waiting area offered a chance to explore video screenings of Aviv's artistic latest portfolio.

Nervous Organ: http://www.orlyart.com/

"Nervous Organ" by Orly Aviv.

The Installation "Nervous Organ" ® © is a video, audio interactive installation powered by sensors. Sophisticated software controls the video/audio system. The visitor enters barefoot into a darkened room (4 to 4 m in size) wired with 35 sensors. The visitor consciously operates two types of sensors: 29 pressure sensors and 6 motion sensors. The pressure sensors were organised on the floor, shaped as electronic keyboard. The motion sensors were connected to the walls. The pressure sensors activate four wide-angle projectors to project 60 video clips on a full-width wall. A reflected floor creates an illusion of a deep ocean environment. The motion sensors activate 6 speakers using 12 pieces of sensual music harmony all over the space. The videos were taken in: aquariums, while diving, and through a submarine that descended to a depth of 400 m (Avi Klapfer). The videos were edited to fit the length of a glance, held for 20 s each. The 12 music clips composed from nature sounds and working harmoniously together to create the illusion of an ocean space: sounds of whale, birds, sea waves, forest wind, bells, and other incidental sounds. The sound clips are played forwards and then backwards.

"Nervous Organ" is a combination of two words with double meanings. Nervous refers to the neurone network of an animal which transmits signals between different parts of its body and in relation to the sensors in the work. Organ refers to the anatomical word for the collection of tissues which serve a common function and relate to the design of sensors installed over the floor. The installation simulates a deep sea diving experience. While diving, the ocean water carries the body and stimulates the senses: hearing, sight, touch, and balance. Observation is done through a mask, which restricts and reduces the range of vision. On land the eye sees over a wide angle; however, looking through a mask, the vision is reduced to a narrow field of vision. Therefore, in order to see a wider range, the diver has to move his entire head. Since the ocean current is constantly moving, each small movement is translated to a full body movement. Each movement opens a new ocean event. The diver—ocean visitor—chooses what, when, and for how long to watch from a specific event. In fact the diver—visitor—sees flashes of images, motion, and sounds. The Installation "Nervous Organ" simulates the above experience.

Videos: Orly Aviv, Avi Klapfer ® ©

Sound: Orly Aviv, Nir Nakav ® ©

Biographical Note

Orly Aviv, digital media artist, has created her own "art-science-technology" distinct style.

Aviv graduated MFA program at the Slade (U.C.L. London, UK). She also holds a BA in Mathematics and Political Science and an MSC in Information Systems. Currently she is working on a research study concerning visual association at the Gonda Multidisciplinary Brain Research Centre with Professor Moshe Bar the head of the Brain Science Faculty. http://www.gondabrain.biu.ac.il/

Aviv uses a wide array of 2D and 3D digital technology. Aviv is interested in the eluded transformation of time to duration and place to space. Her projects display the unceasing variety of physical states, moving our attention from one state to the next. This framed observation of nature exposes internal psychological and philosophical depths. The multiplicity of interpretation of cultural and aesthetic symbols stretches between the absolute and the relative.

Pioneering Computer Art at the Venice Biennale: An Interview with Frieder Nake

Francesca Franco

This interview with Nake, conducted by Franco in 2010 and expanded in 2016,[1] records Nake's recollections of the 1970 Venice Biennale. As discussed in the *Introduction* of this volume, the 35th Venice Biennale, which opened in June 1970, represented a fundamental step for the institution in the long journey towards the acceptance of computer art (Franco 2013). An important antecedent of the 1970 Venice Biennale's experimental exhibition was the first Nuremberg Biennale, curated by the Director of the Institute of Modern Art in Nuremberg, Dietrich Mahlow, in 1969. Titled "Konstuktive Kunst: Elemente und Prinzipien" ("Constructive Art: Elements and Principles"), the exhibition explored the various ramifications of Constructivism up to the present time. One of its sections included early computer-based artworks by Nake and others. The second Nuremberg Biennale, in 1971, was once again organised by Mahlow, this time in cooperation with Janni Muller-Hauck and Eberhard Roters. A section devoted to computer art, "Programmierte Kunst—Computer Kunst", included works by computer art pioneers such as Nake, Georg Nees, and Michael A. Noll.

Francesca Franco: What are your memories of the 1969 Nuremberg Biennale?

Frieder Nake: In 1967, Dietrich Mahlow became director of *Kunsthalle Nuremberg*. His first actions were to rename the old "Fränkische Galerie" and to found an *Institute of Modern Art* as a "scientific sister" of Kunsthalle. A collection of contemporary art was to be brought together, and a new museum building was to

[1] This interview was recorded in London during *Decoding the Digital*, a 2-day conference organised at the Victoria & Albert Museum, on 4th and 5th February 2010 as part of the AHRC-funded project "Computer Art and Technocultures". It was then expanded in 2016 especially for this publication.

F. Franco (✉)
College of Humanities, University of Exeter, Exeter, UK

F. Franco (ed.), *Computational Art at the Venice Biennale (1970–2015)*, Springer Series on Cultural Computing, https://doi.org/10.1007/978-3-032-04258-3_7

become home for both. In 1969 and 1971, Mahlow put up two successful exhibitions of Concrete art as the start of a Nuremberg Biennale. They drew some 125,000 visitors, an extreme success at that time. But Mahlow left Nuremberg in 1971 and the Biennale was discontinued. Both shows included computer-generated works that Mahlow considered necessary elements in the context of Concrete art. His 1969 show became a conceptual and material preparation for an experimental show at the 1970 Venice Biennale of which he was one of the curators.

After leaving Nuremberg, Mahlow extended his curatorial work on the international level. He worked for UNESCO in Latin America. I have tried to again get in touch with him. I wanted to get certain data from him for our *compArt* database (http://dada.compart-bremen.de), but he never answered. I met him only briefly when in 2005 he came to the opening of Georg Nees' exhibition at Kunsthalle Bremen.[2]

FF: What are your memories of the 1969 Nuremberg Biennale?

FN: As I have already mentioned, the 1969 show included some computer-generated works by Mahlow's friend, Georg Nees. I am not sure whether I went to see the show. I don't remember if I had anything in it. After the 1970 Venice Biennale where Mahlow had invited me to participate, he prepared for his second Nuremberg Biennale and invited me to contribute. Quite understandably, he did not like the term "computer art". At that time, it was the term usually used, but it was a term that most of us rejected. Others had been used occasionally, like "computers and randomness", or "programmed art". Mahlow preferred "concrete art" because it was well established.

For the 1970 Venice Biennale, the three curators came up with the fantastic title "Proposte per una mostra sperimentale"—Proposal for an experimental exhibition. In some way this foreshadowed post-modern thinking: just calling something you were actually setting up a proposal. In a sense, they were saying, "we are not making any statements, we just propose".

By the time, I thought that's somehow cowardly—why so cautious? Looking back I now like the title very much.

Even though that show in Venice was announced as a "special show", I said to myself, "oh, to contribute to the Venice Biennale, that's a great honour". The show included Russian Constructivists; Swiss Concrete artists like Max Bill; and Computer Art. As limited as it was, I felt: art history is happening! Since computer-generated works were put into a strong perspective with those other works, it was clear to me that now the computer stuff had been accepted by art history—at least by the world of art. If "Proposals for an Experimental show" was accepted by the Venice officials, then algorithmic art was accepted into the world of art.

As you see, my memories of the 1969 Nuremberg show is almost zero, and it is not much stronger for the 1971 show. Between the two, it is the Venice exhibition that I remember better. But let me tell you of another story, a bit earlier, but with impact for even later.

[2] Mahlow passed away in Darmstadt, Germany, in 2013.

In 1968, I arrived in Toronto for a fantastic year with Leslie Mezei at the Computer Science Department of the University of Toronto. Only a few days after arriving, at a demonstration against the War in Vietnam, I got to know a student of Law with whom I soon became close friends. He kept asking me throughout the year: "How can you, with your political convictions, justify what you are doing at the university, i.e. developing programs for computer art?" Don't you see the contradiction, he insisted to know? In our long discussions, I found my defensive arguments less and less convincing. They always left me with feelings of weakness and insecurity.

I loved what I was doing at the university. I was designing a daring and, I believe, a far-out programme. I was trying to do the best of what we called "generative art". You could input some quantitative conditions that the work of art had to satisfy. The conditions were numerically defined criteria of information aesthetics. In terms of mathematics, it was not a trivial problem. I solved it and was proud of it. But my friend's questions were haunting me. About a year later, early in 1970 (by now I was in Vancouver) I felt that what Max Bense, Abraham Moles, and others were doing as *informatics aesthetics* was wrong.

I had tried to take seriously what they did and attempted to put what they had come up with in information aesthetics into a programme of generative aesthetics. But I was not satisfied by the results.[3] I no longer believed this was exciting against the background of art history. My conclusion became: I had proved that Information Aesthetics is wrong.

My hopes had been that my programme would be creating more exciting results. It would make sense, I wanted to show, that quantitative criteria were an alternative to subjective judgements about pictures. However, in the end I believed this was totally wrong. You can produce something, and do good algorithmic work, but keep in mind that the final judgment always remains with the subject. But I felt, if my programme is going to do well, it will become a commercial thing that I definitely do not want to be part of.

In Toronto, spring 1969, not at the university but at some institution related to the university I gave an evening seminar, "Evenings Information Aesthetics" or some such. The artist Norman White attended. And I believe nowadays that what I told them, they probably thought "That guy is crazy!" Nobody then told me, and they kept coming, so that was friendly. And I was somehow proud. I still believed in this message "we are looking at the work of art first as a sign, then it is made up of pieces, then we add up colours, we measure information, content and so forth". And I believed the programme I had created was very powerful because it incorporated all the information aesthetics measurements I knew of. And I guess in that seminar I probably talked about it. So they must have thought against the pragmatics of North Americans, this guy is crazy. Last year the artist Norman White received the digital arts award and came to Bremen and had a show there, and he told me, "You know what? I took your seminar in Toronto, which then started my long lasting

[3] One of the images generated this way is in Museum Abteiberg in Mönchengladbach, Germany.

career in digital art". So really, in one word, that time between 1968 (arriving in Toronto) and 1970 (the Venice Biennale) is probably a time of deep contradictions in what I did and how I felt.

I would love to hear Auro Lecci, the Italian concrete artist using computers at that time, talking about that! To me, his works then appeared to be boring in some way, too simple, too systematically constructed. They were constructive art, no doubt. They were in the tradition of constructivist art, clearly without any random elements. His work was so different that I would like to hear him talk about that period.

FF: I wonder how many artists that you knew at the time were as politically involved as you?

FN: From what I remember, I may well have been the one most aware of the political situation and its development. Herbert Franke? No, probably not really interested in politics. Georg Nees? Neither. Auro Lecci? I don't really know, maybe? The Croatians and other Yugoslav artists in Zagreb made only little use of computers, but they were politically much more conscious. However, for them computers were in the background—they were more interested in kinetics. I thought differently.

FF: What happened then when personal computers became available in the early 1980s? Did that have an influence on your work?

FN: With the appearance of PCs, computers became commodity products. That caused a totally new situation. To use a computer—"in a room only for the high priest to enter"—required a great amount of expertise. I felt I had that expertise. Now it became possible for everyone to buy such a thing of great computing power. When the programming language BASIC appeared, we, the *experts*, thought of it as really bad quality. At the same time, in 1984, Apple came up with the Macintosh and software like Painter. In consequence, we lost our status of experts. This was, of course, only for software of low complexity, of an everyday functionality.

FF: What did you do after Toronto?

FN: I first went to Vancouver, but returned to Germany in the summer of 1972, to Bremen. In May 1970, still in Canada, I announced in PAGE that "I will stop doing computer art". In October 1971, again in PAGE, I announced, "There should be no computer art". My reasons for this were political and ethical. Indeed, for 12 years I engaged in politics. As a professor of computer science, I was teaching standard computer science. But I withdrew from the field of computer art until I realised that the movement of the New Left had lost its power. In 1985, I wrote a theoretical article for a communist cultural magazine, entitled "What is more important: product or process?"[4] This became the starting point for my slow return back into the field.[5]

[4]The paper was in German, in *Umbruch* June/July 1985, pp. 35–46.

[5]A second paper followed in *Umbruch* Spring 1987, pp. 44–52: Void of sense. Artificiality and computers.

FF: So did you keep in touch with your contacts in Zagreb, where artists were more politically involved?

FN: Loosely only. I always regretted a bit what I had done even though I had done it out of a deep conviction. But those people in Zagreb were my friends. I admired them for their art, for their positions. Much later, I met Matko Mestrovic again, also Ivan Picelj. Mestrovic didn't even remember me, Picelj did.

Darko Fritz became important, an artist/curator from a younger generation. Now I have good contacts again with those who still survive. But during those 12 years from 1972 to 1984, I was in one of the Maoist parties, always a bit in danger. Several times, I was taken to court for political reasons. I don't regret any of this, and I never withdrew.

Much later, it must have been in the 1990s, I started to develop a new positive attitude towards algorithmic art. Looking back, I now I like it much, because I could link this up with an initiative we had started in 1967 in Stuttgart. A group of young assistants had written a memorandum to the officials of the University of Stuttgart requesting that a study programme in computer science should be established. By the time, no computer science department existed in West Germany. Our first proposal contained the unknown position that, besides mathematics, computer science should be based on semiotics.

This position had, of course, no chance to be realised. But it identifies a second root of my relation to computing. I have never given up the claim that computing is a kind of technical semiotics, and during the last 10 or 20 years, this has become obvious. You can view computer science as a sort of *semiotic engineering*, and computer art is one particular application of it. Max Bense's view of aesthetics, as the investigation of sensually perceiving complex signs, nicely links up with my view of computer science, as the investigation of computable processes of signs. And obviously, matters of HCI (Human Computer Interaction) are matters of perception and, thus, of aesthetics.

Biographical Note

Francesca Franco, PhD, is a UK and Italy-based curator, art historian and producer. She researches early computer art and its pioneers, with books including *Generative Systems Art* (2018), and *The Algorithmic Dimension* (2022). Notable curatorial projects include *Vera Molnár: Icône 2020* at the 59th Venice Biennale, *Algorithmic Signs* (Venice, 2017), and *Vera Molnár: Variazioni Icône* (Rome, 2023). She has commissioned significant new works, such as Molnár's first glasswork in Murano, *Icône 2020* (2021), Roman Verostko's *St Mark's Apocalypse* (2017), and Ernest Edmonds's *Growth and Form* (2017). She is Visiting Professor at KIT Karlsruhe Institute of Technology and 2025 SIGGRAPH Art Gallery Chair.

Reference

Franco, Francesca, "The First Computer Art Show at the 1970 Venice Biennale. An Experiment or Product of the Bourgeois Culture?" in *Relive Media Art Histories*, Cubitt, S., and Thomas, P. (Eds.), Cambridge, Mass.: The MIT Press, 2013, 119–134.

Art and Technology at the Venice Biennale, 1968–1970

Francesca Franco

Introduction

Contemporary art in Venice has had a relatively long history that dates back to the first Venice Biennale in 1895. But the first Biennales had a tendency of celebrating the official academic style, or "salon art". They were far from being innovative, and they had a conservative attitude towards art.

However, this original character of the Biennale gradually changed. Particularly in the early twentieth century, with the introduction of the "national commissioner", which is more or less what we now call the curator of the foreign pavilions.

But it is also the introduction of new technologies in art from the mid 1960s that helped the Biennale to take distance from its original nineteenth-century "Salon art" model.[1]

Breaking the Tradition: The 1968 Biennale

It is at the peak of the students' revolt, in 1968, that the Venice Biennale underwent a transformation that instigated the reputation of the Biennale as we know it today.

[1] For an account on art and technology at the Venice Biennale particularly focused on 1970, see Franco, Francesca, "The First Computer Art Show at the 1970 Venice Biennale. An Experiment or Product of the Bourgeois Culture?" published in Relive Media Art Histories, Cubitt, S., and Thomas, P. (Eds.), Cambridge, Mass.: The MIT Press, 2013, 119–134.

F. Franco (✉)
College of Humanities, University of Exeter, Exeter, UK

F. Franco (ed.), *Computational Art at the Venice Biennale (1970–2015)*, Springer Series on Cultural Computing, https://doi.org/10.1007/978-3-032-04258-3_8

During that year, both in Europe and the United States, students, activists, intellectuals, and workers formed movements to demonstrate against capitalism and the bourgeoisie. These protests deeply affected Italy and Italian cultural structures. Many universities were occupied by protesting students as they were conceived as symbols of bourgeois culture. One of the most acrimonious revolts, known as the "Battle of Valle Giulia" (Battaglia di Valle Giulia), took place at the Faculty of Architecture in Rome on 1st March. The Venice Biennale and other art institutions such as the Milan Triennale were boycotted.

The opening of the Biennale in the Summer of 1968 took place in a climate of tension that followed the heated demonstrations of Spring. Students from all over Europe—Rome, Berlin, Amsterdam, and Paris—joined the Venetian group of students who were planning to organise a rally against the Biennale. The students of Accademia di Belle Arti of Venice—occupied since February 1968—and some of their teachers, including painter Emilio Vedova, had planned to bring the battle against the "commodification of art" and capitalism to the Giardini and the Biennale. In order to boycott the Biennale, considered as a "luxurious knick-knack destined to the pleasures of the dominant class", the students invited German student leader Daniel Cohn-Bendit, also known as "Dany the Red"—an icon of the French student rebellion—to participate in the revolt. Support was also expected from the workers of Porto Marghera, Venice's main chemical oil refinery.

In June 1968 flyers signed by "The Committee of Students, Workers and Revolutionary Intellectuals for the Boycott of the Biennale" spread around Venice messages such as "The Biennale is Capitalist" and "No to the Biennale of the Bosses". Another leaflet accused the Biennale of being "the instrument of the bourgeoisie to codify a policy of racism and cultural underdevelopment for the commercialisation of ideas". In Campo della Carità, where the Accademia di Belle Arti was based, posters blamed the Biennale for being responsible for the "mystification of the art production, organisation and control of a culture retained by the dominant class" and promised that "the protest will turn into battle on 18 June, in the occasion of the [Biennale's] opening day, when the culture of the Capital will become market".

On June 18, a crowd of students gathered in Piazza San Marco in order to assault and occupy the Biennale. On that day soldiers from the National Public Security Unit were sent to Venice to guard its wharfs and Piazza San Marco. When the group of protesters started to walk forward, holding signs against the police, a call of a trumpet gave the riot squads the order to attack the protesting crowd.

Artists Emilio Vedova and music composer Luigi Nono supported the students' battle. Artist Giangiacomo Spadari, who took active part in the students' riot, was carried away by three police officers. The police, armed with clubs, violently attacked students and demonstrators. The Police attack was not only directed towards protesters but to anyone in the vicinity of the riots. This included many journalists, tourists, and the commissioner of the Biennale's Swedish Pavilion.

To maintain order the police occupied the Giardini where the Biennale's opening was about to take place. Because of the presence of the police, most of the artists participating in the Biennale refused to open their pavilions. This is what happened in the French pavilion where artists Nicholas Schöffer, Jean Dewasne, and Piotr Kowalski decided to close their gallery space. A similar gesture took place in the Swedish pavilion.

In a sign of protest, artists had covered their canvases before the official delegation arrived to visit the pavilions. None of the artists were present. Some of their works were wrapped and tied up with strings; some works were covered with bed linen, others with black paper. A number of canvases were turned towards the walls, and sculptures were covered up. Eventually, and slowly, the tension decreased and the pavilions of the Biennale reopened their doors.

From a curatorial perspective, the 1968 Venice Biennale represents an "anomaly" compared to its previous editions. It was not only the political stands brought forward by the student revolt but also the introduction of new technologies in art from the mid 1960s that contributed in allowing the Venice Biennale to take distance from its original nineteenth-century salon art model and to open up towards a younger generation of artists and new media. Owing to innovative and cross-disciplinary projects such as those presented by Argentinean artist David Lamelas and French cybernetic artist Nicolas Schöffer at the 1968 Biennale, the institution started, slowly, to embrace new media and to accept them as a new form of art. This, as I would like to argue, had a strong influence in the curatorial directions the Biennale took after 1968.

Lamelas was an exceptional young artist when he participated in the 1968 Venice Biennale—only 22 at the time of the exhibition—with a politically radical work on the Vietnam War titled Office of Information about the Vietnam War at Three Levels: Visual Image, Text, and Audio. The work was an installation representing an office cubicle delimited by glass walls, with Olivetti furniture, a tape recorder, and a telex machine connected to ANSA, the main Italian news agency. The telex machine received constant ANSA updates on the Vietnam War. An assistant was hired to collect the news from the telex during the show, pin them on the wall, and read them aloud to the audience in six different languages, which was simultaneously recorded on tape. Recordings of these updates on the war could be listened to again by the spectator via headphones. The piece marked the introduction of time-based elements and non-traditional media to Lamelas's work, in an attempt to offer the audience an alternative picture of the Vietnam War via neutral, non-emotional audio and visual material.

The works presented by Schöffer in the French pavilion aimed at looking at the effects of movement through interactive sculptures and light environments. Works included a number of pioneering kinetic pieces such as Lux 9 and 10 (1959) made of stainless steel; Microtemps 29 and 33 (1967), that are boxes of wood where stainless steel disks and plates rotated, and where each movement is determined by a programmed electric engine; and other installations and immersive environments where elements made of mirrors, steel, wood, plastic, and electrical dials created a series of dynamic reflections. As French Pavilion curator, Michel Ragon, stated in the introduction of the French Pavilion's catalogue, Shöffer's works represent "the poetic of the machine and light, the poetic of the mechanical movement and cybernetics, and the poetic of electronics. Nicholas Shöffer is the promoter of kinetic art and of the combination of art and science".

The 1968 Biennale's prizes were awarded according to nationality instead of the traditional categories of painting and sculpture. Shöffer and Bridget Riley won the Biennale's Grand Prizes for Foreign Artists. The two Grand Prizes for Italian Artists went to Pino Pascali and Gianni Colombo. These prizes were the last Grand Prizes ever to be awarded at the Biennale. According to a statement published by the Biennale in June 1969, "The official prizes that were previously awarded by an International Jury are from now on abolished, starting from the 1970 Biennale's edition". This choice lasted for over 20 years, until 1986 when new prizes, the Golden Lions, were introduced.

The abolition of Prizes from the Biennale's charter was one of the first palpable effects of the 1968 revolts. A series of debates on the future of the Biennale took place in Venice during that winter, where the institution took into consideration the idea of re-writing its charter in order to reflect the needs of contemporary art and society. The new charter was officially approved by the Italian Chamber of Deputies and senate in July 1973.

The change of the Biennale's original charter was also motivated by the crisis of medium specificity brought to the art scene by the new experiments in art and technology of the early 1960s. This change was anticipated before at the 1966 Biennale, when the idea of challenging the conventional art categories was mooted by kinetic and optical artists, and Argentine artist Julio Le Parc, presented at the Venice Biennale by French art gallerist Denise René, won the Biennale's Best Painting Prize with his kinetic works, which included moving panels with optical patterns to be arranged by the spectator. The award of such a prestigious prize to an artist who encouraged the spectator to play with his works caused considerable criticism among art critics. Comments reflected mixed feelings, including some of amusement and surprise, but also perplexity and confusion over the Best Painting Prize being given to an artist whose works "do not have any paint on it at all".

Following the turmoil caused by Le Parc's award, and the artist's provocative exhibition, the notion of art at the Biennale was undermined, and categories in the visual arts sector became pointless.

1970

The 1970 Biennale represented a fundamental step for this art institution in the long journey towards the acceptance of computer art. In the international context computer art exhibitions were flourishing. Just to name a few important examples, there was Cybernetic Serendipity in London in 1968, but also Event One organised by the Computer Arts Society (CAS) in 1969; and the New Tendencies (NT) movement in Zagreb with a series of exhibitions that they organised from 1961 until 1973.

An important antecedent of the 1970 Venice Biennale was the first Nuremberg Biennale in 1969. The exhibition was curated by Dietrich Mahlow, Director of the

Institute of Modern Art in Nuremberg, and took place in various locations in Germany between April and August 1969. The Nuremberg Biennale, titled "Constructive Art: Elements and Principles" ("Konstuktive Kunst: Elemente und Prinzipien"), featured several sections focusing on the various ramifications of constructivism. It included sections on Russian constructivism, Bauhaus, De Stijl, Suprematism, and computer art.

The section on computer art was inaugurated at the Nuremberg Kunsthalle in June 1969. Among the featured artists were Russian artist Francisco Infante, who since 1962 had been engaged in geometric and then kinetic art, and was later involved in establishing a group of artists and engineers under the collective name Argo (Argo Group of Artists and Engineers, 1970); computer art pioneers Georg Nees and Frieder Nake, who presented their computer graphics both at Nuremberg (1969) and at the 1970 Venice Biennale; and Auro Lecci, who also featured in the Tendencies 4 (1968/69) and Tendencies 5 (1973) Zagreb exhibitions. Other artists included François Morellet, Julio Le Parc, Jesús Rafael Soto, Nicolas Schöffer, and Jean Dewasne.

The 1970 Venice Biennale

The 1970 Biennale opened with the aim of offering to its public an experimental approach to art. The main pavilion, a wide exhibition space covering most of the Giardini's area, housed the show Proposals for an Experimental Exhibition (Proposte per una Esposizione Sperimentale). Curators were Umbro Apollonio, Director of the 1970 Biennale, and Dietrich Mahlow, Director of the Institute of Modern Art in Nuremberg and curator of the first Nuremberg Biennale (1969).

Umbro Apollonio underlined the new experimental approach of the Biennale by proposing "Research" as the main theme of the 1970 event. This, according to the Director's statement in the 1970 Biennale catalogue, was a choice led by the changes that technology brought to society in the previous decade. According to Apollonio, new technologies have brought a new way of understanding events, including the artistic and aesthetic ones, that does not accept a contemplative attitude anymore, but it requires a more active one.

Following these directions, a number of curators invited artists to experiment with new materials and the latest technologies in art. So, for example, the pavilions of Israel, the Netherlands, and Argentina featured works inspired by the latest technologies available.

The Argentinean Pavilion presented a one-man show of the work of young artist Luis Fernando Benedit. Benedit focused his work on animal and vegetal behaviour to create metaphors on the relationship between science and art. For the Venice Biennale, Benedit created an artificial environment called Biotron, a large cage made of Perspex that housed 4000 bees. Bees were fed through a mechanical engine that supplied, through artificial flowers, a sugary solution creating a microhabitat where bees could live and multiply.

The Dutch Pavilion is a very interesting example. Here, architects Jan Slothouber and William Graatsma—founders of the Centre for Cubic Constructions in Holland—used the computer to design a series of modular shapes inspired by the cube using different materials, like concrete, Perspex, and steel. One result was the creation of a series of tiles placed side by side that created an undulated pavement. Each tile was made of concrete and could take the form of a three-dimensional arched element inspired by the cube. Other creations inspired by the same cubic modules were a series of sculptures made of wood, stainless steel wire, and fibreglass.

1970 "Ricerca e Progettazione"

The main pavilion housed the large-scale exhibition "Research and Planning. Proposals for an Experimental Exhibition". The main inspiration of the show was based on two ideas. One was the notion of the "active and conscious spectator", an idea clearly influenced by the 1968 student revolts opposed to the past contemplative inclination of the viewer. The other was the notion of art without categories, due to the recent adoption of new technologies in art since the late 1960s and a consequence of the big turmoil caused by Julio Le Parc's Biennale award in 1966 where he won the best Painting price for a series of "mixed media" works that did not have anything to do with paint at all.

Some of the displayed artworks using computer-generated programmes included Return to a Square by the Computer Technique Group (CGT); Electronic Graphics by Herbert W. Franke; works by Auro Lecci; Matrix Multiplication by Frieder Nake; Computer Graphics by Georg Nees; and a computer-generated sculpture by Richard C. Raymond. Two documentaries on the way computers could be exploited in art were also displayed in the same pavilion.

Another attempt for the Biennale to get closer to its public and give the audience the opportunity to be more "active", or give them a glimpse of the supposed democratisation of art, was the installation of a permanent graphic/printing workshop. Twenty-six artists in groups of four were always present in the workshop to give demonstrations and to help the "active spectators" to create their own artworks by means of serigraphy, lithography, or Xerox machines, and to create sculptures using plastic materials.

A 3-day symposium on the recent developments on digital computer music was also organised by the Biennale in June 1970 at Palazzo Papadopoli. During the symposium Pietro Grossi presented his recently developed project, DCMP—Digital Computer Music Program.

At the 1970 Venice Biennale, Grossi introduced to the audience the Digital Computer Music Program (DCMP), a system through which a computer could read and process musical scores. DCMP was a novelty in the Italian art sector, and, as

Grossi explained during his presentation, it could be exploited creatively in music by anyone. During the symposium, Grossi gave public demonstrations on how the computer, fed via punch cards, could execute any given music score. The machine was also able to process any musical score and randomly play its notes to create new sounds and compositions.

Conclusions

One of the key aspects that have had a significant role in shaping the Venice Biennale's institution—and likewise its curatorial model—since its foundation has been that of national politics. By being a state-funded organisation, the Biennale has mirrored the political changes that have characterised the Italian historical landscape throughout the years. This aspect has had many repercussions on the institutions, both aesthetically and structurally. Owing to the Biennale's ever-changing nature, its curatorial projects have offered a miniature reflection of the broader changes that happen in the world at large.

However, it is also the introduction of new technologies in art from the mid 1960s that contributed in allowing the Venice Biennale to take distance from its original nineteenth-century "salon art" model.

Owing to innovative and cross-disciplinary projects such as those presented by Argentinean artist David Lamelas and French cybernetic artist Nicolas Schöffer at the 1968 Biennale, the institution started, slowly, to open up towards new media and to accept them as a new form of art. This had a strong influence in the curatorial directions the Biennale took after 1968, the major example being the 1970 Venice Biennale and its experimental show.

The Biennale's openness to new media was possibly motivated by its desire to demonstrate its closeness to its public and its democratic position, especially after the students' revolts in 1968. Accepting and showing art and technology there was also a way to find a solution to the Biennale's internal crisis over the renewal of its program. The positive attitude towards technological art represents a rather unusual case in the history of the Biennale. Later attempts to bring art and technology at the Biennale, especially from the mid 1970s onwards, would most of the time be associated with radical-chicness and recuperated by the Biennale on different levels, as I'm trying to investigate in my current research.

The 1968 Biennale, and even more the 1970 experimental show there, were two big "anomalies" in the history of the Biennale, and they demonstrated—for the first time in Venice—that new media art could offer a vital function, or a purpose, of art in society.

Biographical Note
Francesca Franco, PhD, is a UK and Italy-based curator, art historian and producer. She researches early computer art and its pioneers, with books including *Generative Systems Art* (2018), and *The Algorithmic Dimension* (2022). Notable curatorial

projects include *Vera Molnár: Icône 2020* at the 59th Venice Biennale, *Algorithmic Signs* (Venice, 2017), and *Vera Molnár: Variazioni Icône* (Rome, 2023). She has commissioned significant new works, such as Molnár's first glasswork in Murano, *Icône 2020* (2021), Roman Verostko's *St Mark's Apocalypse* (2017), and Ernest Edmonds's *Growth and Form* (2017). She is Visiting Professor at KIT Karlsruhe Institute of Technology and 2025 SIGGRAPH Art Gallery Chair.

Planetary Network at the 1986 Venice Biennale: The Australian Node—An Interview with Paul Thomas

Francesca Franco

This chapter emerges from a wide-ranging conversation with artist and researcher Paul Thomas, whose longstanding engagement with media art—both as practitioner and theorist—continues to offer valuable insights into the evolving landscape of art and technology. The interview took place online over two separate sessions, on 16 and 18 December 2024. Centred on the 1986 Venice Biennale, the conversation revisits one of the most important curatorial projects of the 1980s in the context of media art at the Biennale, offering a rare first-hand account of its development and legacy.

The dialogue explores themes that are not only central to Thomas's practice but also deeply relevant to the broader history of digital and generative art—especially within the context of artistic integrity, institutional expectations, and the fragile futures of digital preservation.

Our discussion begins with a reflection on the tensions many artists face when navigating the demands of funding bodies or institutional frameworks. Thomas underscores the importance of maintaining artistic integrity in the face of external pressures, noting how critical feedback, while often valuable, should never compromise the core of an artist's vision. This concern with authenticity and autonomy forms a recurring thread throughout the exchange.

Digital preservation and the challenges of documenting ephemeral or time-based media form another core focus. Thomas discusses his ongoing archival projects, particularly his attempts to recover, systematize, and make accessible a wide array of early digital artworks—many of which have been inadequately preserved. He questions the usefulness of fragmented databases, arguing instead for a curatorial approach that captures the essence of the works themselves rather than reducing them to metadata.

F. Franco (✉)
College of Humanities, University of Exeter, Exeter, UK

F. Franco (ed.), *Computational Art at the Venice Biennale (1970–2015)*, Springer Series on Cultural Computing, https://doi.org/10.1007/978-3-032-04258-3_9

Throughout, Thomas resists the formalities of academic discourse in favour of what he calls an "organic" process of dialogue and collaboration. He expresses scepticism towards ongoing conventional academic meetings, preferring instead informal exchanges that foster genuine connections among artists, curators, and researchers.

Our discussion concludes with an eye to the future—his plans for new projects, including a self-published book, and the ongoing need to rethink how we write, preserve, and engage with the history of art and technology.

In this interview, Thomas offers an artist's perspective not only a snapshot of his current thinking but also a call to reimagine how we reflect on the cultural significance of digital art. His reflections provide a compelling framework for understanding the tensions and possibilities that shape the field today.

Francesca Franco: Paul, thank you so much for joining me today. Your contribution to the Venice Biennale in 1986, and particularly to the *Technology and Informatics* exhibition at the Arsenale, and your involvement with the Australian node of the *Planetary Network*, were ground-breaking. I'd like to explore the inspirations, processes, and impacts of these projects, to better understand their place in history.

Paul Thomas: Right. So—it's a difficult one, because 1986 is quite a while ago. And actually, a lot of things had already been established. In 1983, we had someone come to Australia—and remember, this kind of technology for me was amazing because unlike Europe, we have the tyranny of distance in Australia. So, this guy came out—Tom Klinkenstein—and he went to Sydney first to start this project up, which was "Australia 2003". So, it was about ideas of being 20 years ahead—doing a lot of faxing with various institutions. In Sydney, there was Eric Gidney the person—who organized the fax link up Sydney of the City Art Institute with Perth and Adelaide.

So, I'm just trying to frame it: there was Media-Space in Perth, Western Australia, which was an art group—not an institution, it was not funded—that had experience of using emerging technology. Kinkenstein brought his typewriter to Media-space, and demonstrated connecting to the network by putting a phone in a coupler on top of the typewriter, and then the typewriter sprang to life printing that it was connecting to IP.Sharp in Canada. Then you suddenly got this idea that you were connected—not only to the whole of Australia but to potentially the world. You could communicate.

It's hard to explain the amazement when you live in the most isolated city in the world, and then suddenly you have this kind of technology that can connect you—it's extraordinary.

Now, it was really a telex system—I don't know how much you know about telex, but it meant typing into a computer. There wasn't a server—it would download when someone logged in, and you'd get messages. So each group had a certain codename, so you could identify who was actually communicating. You'd get screeds of printed material coming out from various institutions around the world. And you suddenly realized that strange delay that—now—is sped up. Like, today, when you text someone and they text you back, but then they've already texted something else before you reply, and it's all a bit out of sync. Back then, it was a *huge* delay. So they think that what they've texted you is what you're answering. And then there's this huge confusion about where you are in time and space, with this just short delay. Well, this was like a *huge* delay. And it was also using telephone lines as well, and using the ASCII code. So you would have to dial up with a modem.

I didn't know anything about network technology, and another member Media-Space Allan Vizents and myself had computers—we decided that we would get a modem, and sign up to ARTEX. So then we were part of this network. And in typing up to ARTEXT, you became involved with a lot of other institutions, and especially Roy Ascott—who I think came out in 1986 to Australia—and I invited him through the ARTEXT Network to come to Perth.

So it was a very exciting time for me personally to be involved, but it was also quite intimidating in some ways as well. Because it's a written format and you can't make mistakes. You're typing to these people about ideas that you might have, that you might be almost embarrassed about, because you're thinking: "Well, A, I haven't spelled it right. B, the grammar's not very good. And I wonder what they're thinking about what I'm writing".

And you might not get a response to it. So I'm just trying to set that kind of scene: that I was in Western Australia, and the institution that set this up—that has that book—was in Sydney.

FF: That's great. And it's a nice companion to this because I've got the catalogue of the exhibition in front of me, with your name in it. [...] So when you say that you felt a bit worried about the results and how it came about, does that mean that there were a lot of expectations?

PT: No, no. It's just because it was so new. It was very complicated—it's very hard to send images out at that time, unless you had a fax machine. They were all done with an Apple Mac and a thing called MacVision. I think it was on MacVision, anyway—it was a thing where you plugged a video camera in and it did a slow scan down the screen to give you a digital photograph that you could send off via fax.

So most of my work in that was taking bits of newspaper, I think at the time, and typing things in that would have been fed into the general news that was going on into the central place in Venice where these texts would be displayed.

So it's always difficult to imagine that, because you already had Roy's *La Plissure du Text 1983*, that were there, and you had another number of projects that were happening. They were becoming quite prolific, to trying to get images. I ran into technical difficulties—especially because you had to change the code of the image from a pixel to codecs like Kermit and then onto binhex, which I can't remember which way round now—before you could get it into a format compressed enough to send it down the phone line.

And sometimes that file would only get to Melbourne, and then you'd get a bounce back.

And it was just *you* in your room at night, trying to log on to be part of something where you don't have to be in real time. Because it's not real time. That's why you always see the photographs of the organizer at the other end—they're always on the phone talking to the participants. They're always trying to confirm what's actually happening, about where they are, how the technology is working.

And not having institutional support meant that we did it by ourselves.

So suddenly you're feeling that you are part of something, feeling that you're connected but also being intimidated, because you felt that it's hard to make a contribution to something when you are miles away in another room, and you've got nothing else around you that contextualizes it. You don't have any infrastructure. You don't have a fax machine and stuff like that. So you haven't got it—it's just you and your computer getting in touch with Venice. And it seems really exciting but at the time strangely alien.

But to some extent you also dealt with a lot of stuff coming back down at you.

I mean, when you look at that—it used to be a very common thing. So that kind of thing there—you see that? *[PT points to an image on a shared screen]*

FF: Yes, that's beautiful.

PT: Yeah—[that's an image] where they make them out of just typing, because that's the only way you could send an image like that. You had to type each one of those letters, and then do the spacing. And making mistakes was so easy to do.

FF: Did it seem like something technologically super advanced at the time, to translate an image like that into a message?

PT: No, not really. It was just by using the keyboard—you were using the space bar to create an image. I remember getting one from a university—I think it was in Hawaii—they did a rocket ship made out of the word "Aloha". It maybe took 20 min for the printer to download, and you'd just sit there wondering what it was. And then—there it is! That kind of anticipation was exciting. Whereas the fax machines would churn out a lot of images—a great medium that was easy to use. Fax machines were really accessible, and you could often get sponsorship from a fax company. Most of the time, for me, it was text. I'm happy for you to have this ["Sydney in Venice—1986"—collection of scans that were sent to Venice during Planetary Network]. There were only about 20 of these made, I think. When you look at those early images—there's a kind of nostalgia there.

FF: Wow thank you, that's such a historical document. By looking at it, it feels a bit nostalgic. In the page you are showing me right now, it says: *This book was printed by Bob at the Sydney College of the Arts, Advanced Education. Compiled by Jan Birmingham, August 1986. 30 copies.* So yeah—really, really important piece of history.

PT: Yes, it is—And Simon Penny is in there too. He was living in Sydney at the time, so he had a few contributions. You can see the "MacVision" heading—that Apple format. They were just using that, and because it was slow-scan, you could do things like with a photocopy. When you put something on a photocopier and the light moves across it? If you go with the light, you can make visually interesting things happen. That's what you'd do—you'd move from one side to the other, or you'd look one way and then the other, and suddenly your eyes had gone. So it was live.

FF: Did being part of such a forward-thinking project change how you viewed technology's role in art?

PT: Absolutely. It stayed with me. It was a very seductive moment to do this. When Artex began to fade—for me, anyway—I put that energy into education. I tried to bring the first computers into the art school. But for me, the key idea was the collapse of space. Allan Vizents and I started going around to see if we could get all the other art spaces in Australia linked into Artex. We wanted a network bulletin board where artists could share and post ideas, so if an artist was visiting, everyone would know about it. It was very simple, but a lot of people resisted it. They didn't want money going into technology when it could go directly to artists.

FF: That tension sounds very familiar....

PT: Yeah, it's really the history of media art. You couldn't show your work anywhere. Curators didn't know what to do with it. Even at Venice in 1986—imagine trying to say, "We want to plug in all these computers to a network". They'd just say, "Where?" There weren't even network cables in the space. And a lot of media art—especially telecommunications art—needs darkness to project or transmit. So when galleries privilege clean white space and light, you're already in conflict with the whole institution. There is a book—*Art + Telecommunication*. It's full of photographs and documents from these projects, although it only goes up to about 1984. There's a fantastic paper in there by Roy—he really knew how to write.

FF: Was Eric Gidney involved too?

PT: Yes, he also wrote a couple of really influential papers, Leonardo. He was important within the institution—made a lot happen—and had a very supportive head of school. The book *Art and Telecommunications* includes a contribution from him, Robert Adrian, Tom Sherman, and others.

FF: Do you know how the Venice Biennale came into the project?

PT: I'm not sure exactly how it got involved. I imagine messages were sent out through ARTEX to invite participants. The front of the book has some general information about that. It just says "Sydney venue" and lists the telex machines, the materials, things like that—"Sydney and Venice", "Venice and Sydney". I don't have the original letter from Venice, but I might have one from Roy to Eric.

FF: When did you first meet Roy?

PT: In 1986. I attended an Artex event, and he was coming out to see Eric Gidney. That's a long trip, so I asked him if he'd stop in Perth on the way. He agreed and gave a lecture there. I was totally blown away—really up at the barricades with him. His ideas just resonated deeply, especially in terms of education and expanding what mediums are available to artists. He was making the case that technology belonged on the artist's palette alongside painting and sculpture. We became friends in that particular way you can with Roy—if you spend even two days with him, you feel lucky.

FF: So it was about feeling connected—to the world, and to the now?

PT: Exactly. That's what it was for me. And it wasn't until the Internet really arrived later that this became easier. When *CTheory* came online, that was huge for me. I don't know if you ever used to read it—it had loads of great papers. I'd print them out—Virilio, Baudrillard, all those. I'd put copies in the pigeonholes of artists at work, and then try to get them together to discuss it. That was around 1995, when that kind of sharing became more viable.

FF: Going back to the 1986 Biennale—did the telecommunication project run throughout the whole event, or was there a global happening just at the opening?

PT: That's a good question. I *think* it was 2 weeks, but it's hard to remember exactly. It might be that I'm conflating things. But I think we were trying to send information from where we were, in real time, and that would be part of a shared series. So there was this unfolding timeline where things were happening across locations.

FF: I'm interested to know about your personal experience and how it had a long-lasting impact not only on your work but in the history of the institution. You know, to be in that early moment. I'm fascinated by what you and the whole Planetary Network team did—because it's something that resonates a lot right now.

PT: I only a very small node in the Planetary Network exhibition in that context… Roy had a number of teaching positions before setting up the Centre for Advanced Inquiry in the Interactive Arts. This morphed in to the Planetary Collegium, and all seemed to continue his ideas of doing things network technologies. Roy was running the Planetary Collegium—a group of PhD students who would meet around the world at various locations. It was initially based on the network, but they still had to meet physically. They would travel and meet to discuss these all things. We all used the experience to put back into art education, to critique and explore new modalities of art practice.

FF: Does that experience continue to inspire your work today? Was there a key lesson from it that stayed with you, or still plays a role in how you make art—or how you see art now?

PT: Yeah. Well, I've been working in this area for a long time. I think I started just after 1983—so, you can see this—you can actually download it [http://mass.nomad.net.au/i-send-you-one/]. This is one of my Web sites: *nomad.net*.au. It has a lot of early curricula on it. Curriculum was something I was really interested in. The *I send you one* project here is linked to that. Roy's students worked on it, and a number of others. If you've downloaded the image—I think I sent you one—you'll see it's got that sort of art-text, teletext aesthetic in the background. You'll see names. I'd send them out—and then I'd get images back. I couldn't send images by phone, so I'd put them on a Mac disk and post it. Then they'd send back their own images—interpretations of photographs I'd taken around Perth with a friend. I wish I still had those original images, but this is all I've got left.

FF: I'm scrolling through the images in the PDF now—yes, that's great.

PT: So the influence from that time was definitely there—the ability to affect people at a distance, to touch at a distance. All of that became really important to me. The notion of reconfiguring space. If you look through my Web site, you'll see this constant testing of space, challenging of spatial assumptions.

There was an interesting paper by Lev Manovich on the collapse of space—he compares Benjamin's aura with new technology and the collapse of space, 1996, referencing Paul Virilio. https://manovich.net/index.php/projects/cinema-and-telecommunication-distance-and-aura He looked at those two together, and I thought it was quite good. This sense of connectivity—of feeling connected—was important. But when you read the romantic texts about art and technology from that era—what people thought was going to happen—the poetics of what Roy was imagining... a dream of shared consciousness, a *noosphere*, where you could just reach out and pull information from the air... It was a dream. I don't think anyone ever imagined it would go as badly as it has with technology. It was such a good, such an interesting idea. But it's become so demanding.

FF: I was going to ask—when you think about how connected we are today, maybe *too* connected—do you miss that earlier time, when we weren't constantly connected, but technology was just starting to allow for those connections?

PT: Do I miss it? No, I don't miss it. Because any form of progress is... well, I just think we went wrong. We went wrong on a number of fronts. Take quantum, for example—everything in physics is about the effects of quantum, but not quantum itself. It's all about mathematical outcomes, and nothing about the physical, human relationship to it. You're only ever seeing the outcome of mathematics. And then if you look back to the beginnings of binary code, ASCII code the sending of information, and this massive acceleration...I don't think we ever looked at it in a *highly critical* way—really thought about what was going to happen. Because a lot of the artists were focused on how art would affect it—not so much on what it was doing to art. I mean, you could go back to Duchamp, and his *the Fountains*, and say that that work messed up everything, or you could say it's the greatest artwork, but it seems to fall very nicely into a kind of Capitalist society where people have now factories and teams of people, like in the old masters, and they come and do small touches and they make 20 paintings and they all sell at millions of dollars. The dream has become real, and Capitalism owns it.

In Virilio's *Art and Fear* there's a chapter called "The Pitiless Art"—it's obviously a lecture at some stage that he's turned into a chapter, because he talks about this theorist—Jeanette Lichtenstein. He talks about that... she goes to Auschwitz to see it, and then she goes into the museum, and she says she looks at these objects that are all around—like a baby's dummy and things like this in cases. And she says what she sees is contemporary art. And she comes away from it thinking that *they've won in the end*—because this whole thing has been turned into a kind of art machine. And it's a very aggressive kind of chapter about contemporary art.

So I think that, for me, the network opened up a thing for people that were isolated from this whole thing—from being in a centre like New York or Paris—even though that's still there, and it's still super powerful. It's very hard to... everybody needs a champion to get into the sort of capitalist market. But the network gave—for a short period of time—a platform that was ubiquitous across all fields. A designer uses the computer, this person, scientist, a businessman, accountant—it was all the same screen, it was all the same stuff on the same aesthetic platform. And suddenly, artists could engage in lots of different things with it. But it didn't have the capabilities to go on. And, a place like Venice would maybe take it on as almost a novelty. People were amazed by the novelty of it—like when Facebook is on, and the pair of shoes that you were looking at the other night—there's like 300 different shoes that suddenly come out, and you go, "*How do they know I was looking at shoes?*" People are amazed by the fact that they think the computer knows them. And so that novelty... and then that fetishization of this technology.

So I think we've got a long way to go, with art, just to sort of address it—as opposed to critique it—like the project you did with the glass [PT mentions Vera Molnar's glasswork, *Icône 2020*]. Bringing it back to a different material base in some ways confronts it, but you also get this thing that technology should always be using new mediums. You know, you can't paint a concept of technology. Like, it's very hard if you said, "*My paintings are about technology*" or "*My drawings are about technology*". Unless you're some artist like, for example, Gerhard Richter—who did those screen prints on top of AFM images—where it seems that he's using his technique on top of that scan, and there's some direct context. Well, I mean, there is a context because of the blur—but it's just interesting.

And I don't know the answer to a lot of these things. I just think that for me, it's like the whole notion of temporality. And what the Internet gave us was a different structure of time. It caused us to think about—even to organize our meeting now—to get the time wrong and this wrong… it gave you that sort of real… really thinking about space. About what constitutes a natural interval, about the concepts of intervals, the concept of time—it doesn't exist. So this event exists in time—they're all different, and they're all blurred, and they all have a massive amount of information circulating around them. From what you're going to have for breakfast now, what I'm going to have for dinner, everything—to our bodies, what our minds are thinking about—and we can't even capture, a little bit of that. So how do we express something about it? How do you express something when you've got this *gluttony of imaging* going on all the time? How does an artist make any critical impact into that? You could see with media art that for example when Christa Sommerer and Laurent Mignonneau were doing their plant work—and buy touching the plants you could make the animation evolve—all this now becomes something that you could then make into an app, and then you could put it on your computer, and a company can make a lot of money, having this same process happen that was originated by the artists.

[Communication gets cut off]

FF: It's so funny that our conversation got truncated exactly when we were talking about technology and how connected we are these days.

PT: Yeah. It's so funny.

FF: I was going to ask, just as we got cut off: do you miss those early days before all this developed technology? Compared to now, when we're so connected—do you miss that time?

PT: No, I don't miss it. It's like asking if you miss the time before telephones.

So once you start going back, where do you stop? Do you go back to the early MUD/MOO chat rooms and say, "*I wish we could get away from those?*" Not that everyone was on MUDs and MOOs—it was just a few people. But no, I don't miss it.

I just think we've created something we can't fully comprehend. Like with the atomic world—it's so tiny, so minute, and it doesn't compute with us. We struggle to understand its fundamentals, like the uncertainty principle. And we're connected to that, because we're made of the same materials. At a submolecular level, we're all quantum.

And then you start to think—maybe those kinds of connections existed a long time ago, just without our awareness. Maybe through intuition, or other means. You look at the Surrealists, or Kandinsky, or Blavatsky. A lot of scientists doing "ether physics" were talking about networks, telepathy, and so on.

So I wouldn't presume to go back. I just think we keep going down a technological path—a scientific one. But maybe we need to go down a different path.

Looking at the past, there was a self-consciousness about what to do. You'd be given a kind of fake project, like "*the news*", and you'd find that many people didn't have the time or conceptual framework to address it. So the results could be banal.

Then you had slow scan TV—like an image of me, moving very slowly, and the next frame starts to scan. You try to set up a chat with someone, but it's so stilted that you can't. Your movements, your actions—they become... restricted.

And I suppose the only way forward with the network is to become more introspective about what you're trying to do with it.

I was going to suggest to you that all of this stuff in Venice—what Roy did, for example—was fundamentally conceptual art. They had the technology to make it happen, but they couldn't fully make it happen. But the thing driving it was a beautiful concept: the collapse of space, the idea of being connected to someone.

But then you face the problem of not knowing what to say—as an art piece. Like, if you and I decided to do an artwork together tonight, maybe I'd light a candle and you'd try to blow it out. It would be funny because you couldn't. But it's still very much a conceptual issue. That kind of performative act, done over the Internet, is a lot like a Fluxus performance.

So I think it's steeped in that kind of history and tradition.

I was just listening to this guy give a talk about definitions of art—the institutional definition and all the others that don't really make sense. And he said one comment that really stuck with me. He was talking about Duchamp's *Fountain* and said, "*That urinal wasn't art. It was a comment on art. And a comment on art can't be art*". Whether it's true or not, I don't care—it's a great provocation.

So then you wonder—is all conceptual art just a comment on art? Or is it art from the start because it helped construct the conceptual art movement? And if the urinal predates the movement, then maybe it can't be art, because it's simply a comment.

Then you look at political art—is that art? Or is it something else? Is it about the signature? The fact that it got locked into the canon?

That's what makes me think of the strong link between networking and conceptual art. For some people—including Roy—it was very much about something spiritual. A different state of mind. The idea of being networked together, of shared consciousness.

So when institutions like the Biennale got hold of that early on and tested it, it was fascinating. To position that kind of work in the bastion of the art world was important.

Then you can start to look at other occurrences—how often they happened, how they changed. Which is the kind of thing you're working on.

FF: How does it evolve? Is everything a data projection now? And are the data projections coming from media artists or fine artists? If there's no difference, then we're back to square one. Why are we doing this?

PT: My argument is that media art, or new media art, stopped evolving around 2006.

FF: Why that particular time?

PT: For me, it's an important marker. The Australia Council stopped funding new media art grants around that time. It wasn't that they didn't fund art, but they stopped categorizing it as "new media". Artists had to apply under the broader category of art instead, and they wouldn't receive funding anymore if they specified it as "new media". Of course, this led to artists turning to more hybrid biological art projects, but biological art is its own field—it's not considered new media art. The funding landscape became confused. Then they tried to return to experimental art, but the problem with that was that there were no clear criteria to assess experimental art. Nobody wanted to fund something that was too risky. If you fund something that could potentially go too far, like an experiment where you're trying to shoot a plane down, Chris Burden's Last Stand, it creates huge risks for the government. So, this interim period of confusion about where art and technology meet started to unravel.

FF: So, you're referring to a period when artists first had access to computers that were relatively affordable?

PT: Yes, to me new media art as opposed to media art started around 1980; artists could start getting computers, especially if they had a job to support the cost. But many couldn't code, so software developed to assist visualizing ideas, but there wasn't much theory behind it. At the time, you only had film theorists or photography theorists, and they would apply their frameworks to digital media. If you gave them a screen, they'd try to apply traditional frameworks, saying "this is photography, this is video", without understanding the interactivity of the new medium. So, artists to begin with had to develop their own theory of new media art, and the whole field was in its infancy.

FF: That spiritual aspect you mentioned earlier—do you think it came through and was understood when they showed it at the Venice Biennale? Is it an insight that stuck?

PT: It's a possible insight, but it's very complex. It's like the Schrodinger cat experiment—whether the cat is alive or dead. When a scientist is asked about it, they'll say, "I don't care about that at all. As long as the math works, that's all I care about". It's a way of simplifying the world by ignoring things that don't fit into the formula. It's a method of cutting out 90% of the complexities. The same could be said for how the network evolved. Once it became ubiquitous, it stopped being its own field. For instance, NetArt, which had a short-lived surge in the early 1990s, fizzled out because technologies like WordPress came along and made it easier for everyone to create Web sites, etc. As soon as software became more complex and ubiquitous, it lost its niche.

FF: That's an interesting perspective. My whole PhD dissertation focused on the role of the Venice Biennale in accepting and eventually awarding media art. When I was doing my research, it became clear that the Biennale was one of those places where experimentation happened very rarely. It's a stiff institution, often more traditional than avant-garde. But in 1970, the Biennale did show a more experimental side, especially with its exhibition that included computer art. I find the 1986 Planetary Network at the Biennale particularly interesting in this respect, because it happened precisely when the computer started to become more accessible to everyone…

PT: Right. Around 1983, things started to change. The computer became an equalizer because, no matter who you were—whether an artist or a business—you were using the same output: the screen. The computer opened up a new world for people. You had artists, people from various industries, all using the same medium, and that blurred the boundaries. It was a democratizing moment. Ars Electronica capitalized on this idea of "soft-skilled operators"—people who didn't need formal art training to use technology. They could just jump into the digital realm and start creating. But, as you mentioned, by the late 1990s, the rise of platforms like WordPress made it harder for these new media artists to sustain their niche.

FF: You mentioned the "Aesthetics of Care". How does that connect to this?

PT: Oh yes, I've been interested in it for some time. In 2002, during the Biennale of Electronic Art in Perth (BEAP), Oran Catts hosted a conference called the "Aesthetics of Care". I made sure it was recorded because I believed the event was significant. And just recently, I found those old recordings. Let me play you a part of it. You might not be able to hear it clearly, but I'll give it a try.

[PT plays audio: https://mass.nomad.net.au/beap02-the-aesthetics-of-care-ilecture/]

PT: It was just Laurie Andrews, who was a lawyer for the American government regarding biological issues. When people started becoming further synthesized and they became plants, how would they get a passport? Because they wouldn't be human. So, it's kind of an ethical thing, with things changing and transferring. She was one of the first people to consider this, and she gave a keynote at the Aesthetics of Care conference in 2002.

FF: So do you think those key lessons from the Planetary Network have been, in a way, taken further now?

PT: That's a good question. I think the mainstream art institutions that presented exhibitions were attempting to colonize this burgeoning medium, which to some extent had its roots in Mail Art. At the time, the aesthetics and technical complications of the medium meant that there were no curators with experience in telematic art.

So, I think that Roy's Planetary Collegium PhD programme was a great thing to come from having exhibitions like The Planetary Network Exhibition as part of the Venice Biennale. You know, Paul Sermon, Christa Sommerer, Laurent Mignonneau, Victoria Vesna, and Bill Seaman are just a few examples of the benefits of Roy's telematic philosophy.

Paul Sermon who just recently gave a very funny presentation in Venice [PT mentions Paul Sermon's talk at the 10th Media Arts History Conference, Venice, 2023], like these two people in the car and this sort of virtual pop-up thing. But from the immense complexity of what he first made with *Telematic Dreaming*, the rights of the human to have a digital moral code to what you could do with somebody was self-evident in that work. It breached lots of protocols straight away. To me, it was an amazing piece because of that. It just set up these alarm bells everywhere about what we're doing now—the ability to caress your digital body or something, you know, this invasion of you. There was a famous case in 1993, one of the MUD sites, a multi-user domain network, like telex, where a woman in a group said she was molested by the text [https://research.usq.edu.au/download/e3a84d008f8c4121f9a10ded21ec04242d9df647ea32987f4a01ce7a71fe25d1/93306/Johnson_Refractory_v13.doc.pdf]. People in the group set up a court and tried the person and found them guilty of molesting that person. But none of it made any sense because that person could have been a female or a male. The court could be or couldn't be real? But it was a global thing. So, suddenly you get somebody globally who's charged with rape, and then the network starts to go from a medium that was a dream of potential to suddenly becomes a hostile strange virtual space that you didn't know whether to enter or not. Like all the online scams that happen now. You used to be able to build a Web site where, when pop-up windows first came out, if you had a pop-up window that could open automatically, your screen would just start getting pop-up windows all over it. And you couldn't stop the pop-up windows because you just couldn't stop them. So, that very simple pop-up window became a scam for lots of artists to make artwork that just kept on reiterating that you had to quit the machine to stop the thing from procreating and making lots more of them…

FF: And from your experience, from what you remember, was there anything similar happening in other institutions around the world?

PT: Well, I think lots of people were trying; certain people were trying to model off Roy's kind of work. And in the *Encyclopedia* [PT refers to: Gere, Charlie, Francesca Franco, Paul Thomas, Vincent Dziekan, and Anna Munster, eds. *The Bloomsbury Encyclopedia of New Media Art*. I. II. III vols. London: Bloomsbury Academic, 2025], a lot of the artists that are writing actually went through the *Planetary Collegium*. So, a lot of people mention tangentially, even David Rokeby mentions Roy, but he didn't—he went to the University in Canada where Roy was, just after he had left. With system in place, but he wasn't there. He had a major impact. But when you read his early papers, they were amazing—early papers about the future, about quantum, about bio. When SymbioticA's Oron Catts and Ionat Zurr became part of BEAP 2002, they presented *BioFeel*, a pioneering exhibition of biological art. Roy was asked to open it. And he said, "Finally, we've got moist media, which is great". Then we all went to the cafe afterwards. When Oran and Ionat came in, everybody was clapping and cheering. It was quite a nice experience to set up.

FF: Yeah, I'm asking that because I was so surprised when I visited the Tate exhibition last week, *Electric Dreams*. It's one of those big exhibitions that finally reached a major institution like Tate, and then Roy was missing. It felt really strange.

PT: I think they overlook him because, to some extent, he left behind traditional practice-based art. He was turning more to exploring a telematic research with the *La Plissure du Text* and the integration of technology within the fabric of architecture. You know, Roy was really a future person. And future people don't get…

People who come and do the stuff after the future has been explored—institutions can't catch up that fast with people like Roy because he's like 10 steps ahead of them. Then he becomes someone you can't categorize.

That's the one thing about interactive art that I've always found difficult. I didn't want to allow others to have too much control over the aesthetics of what they see, because I want to be the orchestrator of it, not make everybody else an artist, which is what the technology can do. The ubiquity of technology ended up making everybody the artist.

Contemporary art is a problem. I think the Venice Biennale has been dealing with contemporary art for a long time, but it doesn't make any sense, because everything is always contemporary of itself. It has no criteria by which to say, "As long as it's of this time, then it's contemporary". And so, we've got a museum of contemporary art that can never not be contemporary because it can't suddenly be experimental or anything else because it's contemporary, unless contemporary is of its time now.

FF: Yeah, I think the Venice Biennale, from what I could understand from reading and seeing all the catalogues, has shown the art of its time probably only in 1948 when Peggy Guggenheim showed Pollock...Really great pavilion and then in 1970, but then, I mean, the Venice Biennale started as a commercial.

It started in 1895 when Venice was collapsing. There was this idea of "death in Venice". And so they tried to revive the tourism and the economy of the place through an art exhibition.

PT: Ars Electronica began in 1979. And that was done for the same reason—to reinvent Linz. Because all the resources and the mining had all been closed down, and they needed to reinvent the city, and they did it through technology and through Ars Electronica. Art and Technology like that gets can be strategically used, I tried to get a computer lab in the art school. Very difficult. Graphics had a computer lab, but Fine Art didn't have a computer lab. And so I argued for the computer lab. So they didn't want fine art, but you could make an argument that fine art can now not only make fine art, but they can also be productive in the sense of getting employment because they're trained with adaptable technology. They could become designers, set designers, all these things, and a number of others that use technology through design, through planning. And so you'd make this argument even though you hated the argument, because you wanted the facilities, but you were going down the wrong path. It's like, the Roy's kind of model of education doesn't fit into any institution, really, because they can't budget them.

FF: And it probably proves that art cannot be constricted into institutions anyway or into education. I mean, do you need a degree to be an artist?

PT: No, you don't. But institutional art is something that most artists have been institutionalized, and it's very hard to get rid of that. You know, like my drawings that I've just made, I might have mentioned this yesterday. You feel, compared to the electronic artwork I make, that people think you've left or that you've done something else, even though I see them as making exactly the same contribution. Not exactly, but progressing my understanding of a quantum phenomenon, in a way that I'm trying to explore it through these drawings. You imagine that somebody looking at them, maybe they don't, but somebody looking at them would think, "They're drawings, quantum art should be technologized". If you're going to make it, it should be going through some technological thing, either it has to be didactic to prove something or it has to have some mathematical kind of outcome. Anyway, it's just saying I feel… I don't know if it's true or not.

FF: To me, the medium has to be functional to the message when you make art.

PT: Yes, so when you worked on *Icône 2020*, in glass, and you have that kind of technological pieces behind [PT refers to Molnar's original 1974 plotter drawings that formed the conceptual basis for *Icône 2020*] and then you make it into traditional glass, you're doing something that is in some ways going backwards to a lot of people. So to them you're not progressing the field, you're going into a very, very structured medium and narrative.

FF: And you know the funny thing? To make that glass piece, especially to cut that piece in 100 holes, we used a machine that looked almost exactly like a plotter drawing machine. So it's really funny to think that, yes, in a way it looked like we went backwards with the ancient tradition of glassmaking, but the technique we use was very similar to what pioneer used to make their early works.

PT: Yeah, absolutely. But you see, if it's not done in that kind of narrative form, like if you made it with rapid prototyping out of some unique material that had never been used before, or you made it out of Vantablack, and then the thing was absorbing nearly all light, and suddenly they have this thing. I was thinking a lot about that, because nearly every project I've been involved with, which was in the network in the beginning, there was a lot of questioning, I think because of the aesthetics, because it was not established. A lot of the work was A4 size, especially fax work; it was nearly all A4. For example, I did a collaborative work with Roy's students once where they were faxing images and words on half a sheet to Perth. So my students drew on the other half a sheet in responses, faxed it back across so the other student in Wales who could respond and it could be all mix up. So they both had an identity. But yeah, it's experimental, not something that you would want to show a lot of people.

FF: Going back to Planetary Network. Were you worried about the way the piece will be received by the public?

PT: Yeah, I was worried more self-consciously because I had to write, I couldn't send images so I had to write and I was dyslexic, I was paranoid that I'd be seen as this fake person from Perth that was joining in and he hadn't read a book so he didn't know how to write or even, like one of those movies, where you've seen all the horror movies, so when they do a spoof on them, you know where every bit of the spoof comes from. And I'm going, "Ahhh!" It was very strange, but so yeah, I found it very intimidating, a very intimidating medium.

Even though the information would be presented as a continual stream of information, so I doubt many people would have read my contribution, it has that strange feel of typing into the ether.

FF: It's so nice to hear about this story from your perspective. Because when I was writing about the Venice Biennale, when I was studying it, I had the impression that the Biennale accepted this project just because the computers were starting to become more ubiquitous. So it felt like they accepted that kind of art just when it was a safe time to accept it. But when you tell me about this project, it actually looks as if it was much more than that. So it's really nice still to hear these backstories. And by the way, it's so nice to speak about this project while I'm in Venice and you're in Sydney.

Can you tell me more about the catalogue you mentioned earlier on?

PT: Yeah, I've uploaded one of Roy's projects the *La Plissure du Text* from Sydney. It's available for download [PT points to the link: http://mass.nomad.net.au/la-plissure-du-texte-project-].

FF: This sounds fascinating—So, you're also offering access to some important archival material through your Web site?

PT: Exactly. And here, on the page, you can see a famous Australian artist, Mike Parr. [PT pointing to a photograph]. He's known for very physical performances, like self-induced vomiting and inflicting pain, such as holding his hand over a candle. But he later gave up performance art and shifted to more towards traditional printmaker. The catalogue itself has some interesting artworks, though, I would say, some of them feel a bit raw comparison to today's standards.

FF: It's always fascinating to think about how the perception of art changes over time. How do you think this shifts the role of curators?

PT: It really makes you reconsider the relationship between the idea behind the work and the actual work itself. As a curator, it can be tough to translate something like this into a contemporary context. What we saw back then might not have the same impact today, especially when it's juxtaposed with more polished works. It raises questions about how to view these works in today's art scene.

FF: Absolutely, that's a big question. And I understand you've been involved in several Biennales and exhibitions. Could you tell me more about your experience with the 2004 Biennale?

PT: Yes, in 2004, we did the second BEAP. The theme was about losing identity and denying difference. It was called *The Same Difference*. We had five exhibitions and five conferences, one opening every night with a conference the next day. It was a bit of a logistical nightmare to organize, but it worked because of the five curators involved—each handled a separate aspect of the event. If one part didn't work out, the whole event wouldn't fall apart. It was produced on a small budget, but it had a more intimate feel.

FF: That sounds like a very dynamic approach! You mentioned working with different curators. How did that work out?

PT: It was a good experience, though managing multiple curators can be challenging. Having five separate centres with smaller budgets kept the whole thing flexible. I remember one curatorial decision was to not have curators present the own artistic work. There were concerns about the potential perception of nepotism—some people didn't like the idea of curators being artists themselves. It's a tricky thing to navigate.

FF: That's a really interesting insight into the curatorial process. Do you still keep track of these past events?

PT: Yes, I do! I've got several Biennale catalogues uploaded online; the artists from those exhibitions were really talented. Even though it was a bit chaotic, there was something special about bringing people together. Like you, Francesca, did in Venice for the Media Art History conference, you get this really good buzz having all these people that you knew and liked in the same city, and you brought them there, and it's a good feeling to have, that you've achieved it and made it a physical shared experience that doesn't happen in online spaces. I think that's what makes these in-person events so important.

FF: It must have been such an exciting feeling to have those connections and create such a vibrant event. Speaking of events, you've got a talk coming up, right?

PT: Yes, I'm hoping to be in Venice in May for an AI conference. There's a conference on the ethics and aesthetics of artificial intelligence—AI Venice 2025. It's one of those conferences that's becoming more common now—AI is such a hot topic.

FF: It seems like there's a conference every week now on AI! Do you feel it's a bit overwhelming?

PT: Yeah, it really is. But at the same time, it's great because it shows just how much interest there is in the subject. For me, it's a chance to explore AI in new contexts from a quantum perspective.

FF: Since I worked with Vera, especially on that glasswork, I kind of stopped worrying about how an artwork is perceived—whether it's understood or accepted by institutions. I really stopped worrying about that. I don't know if I was just lucky to work with her, because she was totally unbothered about that. But it felt as if I did something that was really important for myself and for her. And then if people understand that, that's good. If they don't, that's ok, and it doesn't bother me.

PT: I'm 100% with you. I mean, I get hurt about things like that. Like, if somebody says your work or… you know, if you read a review of something and they say something mean about you, then I get hurt. But I actually care but don't care if they see it. Their opinion wouldn't make me change the art that I make.

And so, I still care in some ways, but actually, I'm not going to make my art differently because you don't like it, or you don't like this, or you don't like that. You know, and artists, like, it's when you apply for a grant and you're trying to twist what you're actually doing to fit the grant. I hate that…

It's part of the nomad site. So, something like this, just to get you excited. I tried to get a lot of curricula together and evidence of what was happening educationally and what colleges were doing. This is one of the projects [https://www.nomad.net.au/resources]. So if you look at this, you'll see a whole list of curriculum and other things that I got from doing a scoping study of curriculum. So you've got the resources. If you click on the resources, you can go up to the date. You've got *La Plissure du Text* in there as well. You've got the Digicon night satellite, you've got Australia, you've got the world in 24 h. And you've got some telecommunication research by Bill Bartlett. I can't remember who Bill Bartlett was now. But you also got, to some extent, the history of Sound Art, which really started quite a long time ago.

FF: Are you going to feed all this information into a global database?

PT: Yeah, I mean, I'm happy to go anywhere. But I am not really interested in media art archival stuff. I mean, databases and ownership are very complicated. I proposed a couple years ago to talk about the fact that a lot of artists had their own Web sites. Those Web sites were like an insight into how they thought, and it would be better to collect all those rather than try to link up various databases that aren't going to link up. You know, it costs a fortune to try and get something to write all the code to make these things connect. But it would be much better to set something up to preserve some of the basic HTML that was there at the beginning and some of these things, and try to get Marco Media software like Director and Shockwave, so some of these CD-ROMs and other net artworks could be restored back together and place online.

FF: Yeah, that makes sense. Thank you so much, Paul. It's been great talking to you—fascinating and inspiring as always. Your reflections on the 1986 Venice Biennale and its legacy offer such valuable insights into the evolving relationship between art and technology. I really appreciate the chance to revisit this pivotal moment with you.

https://journals.uvic.ca/index.php/ctheory/about

Biographical Note

Dr. Paul Thomas is an Honorary Professor at the University of New South Wales (UNSW), Sydney. He is the founder and series chair of the International Transdisciplinary Imaging Conference series (2010–2024). In 2000, he founded the Biennale of Electronic Arts Perth (BEAP) in Western Australia and served as its inaugural director in 2002, 2004, and 2007. As an artist, he is a pioneer in transdisciplinary art practice. His practice-led research not only draws inspiration from nanoscience and quantum theory but actively operates within these atomic domains. Thomas's artworks, rooted in scientific research, have been exhibited both nationally and internationally. His recent works focus on capturing glimpses of reality, with his 2022 piece Quantum Chaos exploring the liminal space between the quantum and classical world. He has also led Quantum Drawing workshops at international institutions His academic publications revolve around the idea that probability and uncertainty are fundamental forces at the core of both art and science. His notable works include *Quantum Art and Uncertainty* (2018), *Nanoart: The Immateriality of Art* (2013), and *Reconfiguring Space* (2009). He is currently serving as the editor of the *Encyclopedia for New Media Art, Volume II Artists and Practice*, Bloomsbury.

Planetary Network at the 1986 Venice Biennale: The Venice Node—An Interview with Maria Grazia Mattei

Francesca Franco

This interview, recorded in Milan on 9 June 2025, features Maria Grazia Mattei, Founder and President of MEET, the Italian Center for Digital Culture (Milan). A journalist, art critic, and self-described "digital evangelist", Mattei offers a compelling reflection on the trajectory of new media art and its intersection with technology from the 1980s to the present day. She traces a consistent and visionary path, deeply rooted in early avant-garde influences and a fascination with the social implications of emerging digital tools. Her work has been defined by a commitment to interpreting and making accessible the complex processes of technological innovation within art, emphasizing participation, collaboration, and real-time communication long before these became mainstream concepts.

Throughout the conversation, Mattei highlights the contrast between the rapid embrace of technology by the cinema industry and the slower, more resistant reception within the traditional art world—particularly within Italy's institutionally conservative context. She recalls the hopeful utopian spirit of early telematic art, which repurposed everyday office technologies like fax machines and satellites into instruments of creative exchange and cultural democratization. This spirit anticipated the development of today's interconnected digital society, despite later commercial pressures that complicated its idealistic beginnings.

Mattei also shares her ongoing ambition to curate a major international exhibition dedicated to the vibrant Italian digital art scene of the 1980s and 1990s—an effort to reclaim and articulate the significance of this foundational period in the broader history of contemporary art. Finally, the interview underscores the essential role of public engagement and institutional support in nurturing experimental art forms, reflecting both the breakthroughs and challenges encountered along this remarkable journey.

F. Franco (✉)
College of Humanities, University of Exeter, Exeter, UK

F. Franco (ed.), *Computational Art at the Venice Biennale (1970–2015)*, Springer Series on Cultural Computing, https://doi.org/10.1007/978-3-032-04258-3_10

Francesca Franco (FF): Thank you for being here with me, Maria Grazia. The 1986 Venice Biennale, dedicated to art and science, remains a milestone in the history of the Biennale and in how art and technology were integrated—particularly through the *Ubiqua* project, which you co-curated within *Planetary Network*. How did this project begin? What are your memories of it?

Maria Grazia Mattei (MGM): Well, it was 1986. I had graduated in Art Criticism several years earlier, in the late 1970s. While trying to understand what my future might look like, I went to Rome and found myself in this garage-like space—though it wasn't really a garage, it was a tiny room—belonging to Michele Böhm. I later invited him to the Biennale within the *Planetary Network*. There, I discovered a group of artists and researchers who were working with personal computers to create images.

I remember seeing an animation by Michele Böhm and his group, called *Crudelity Stoffe*. I still remember the name—it left a strong impression on me.

At the time, I was writing for *Zoom* magazine, and I was looking for material related to the use of art in connection with new technologies. Back then, that mostly meant video art and photography. I left photography aside because a friend of mine was covering that for the same magazine, and I didn't want to overlap with her. So I threw myself into video art.

Through my research for *Zoom*, I discovered *Crudelity Stoffe* in Rome. That's when I had a powerful intuition—I said to myself, "The world is going to be digital", and I knew I wanted to focus only on that.

This group had created a software system for animation in which each mark transformed into another by subtraction. Their theory was based on "abolitionism"—meaning subtraction rather than accumulation. Just think how relevant that idea is today, in a world flooded with data and information.

I think that intuition was partly informed by my university studies, where I had focused on the artistic avant-gardes in relation to new technologies. It's always been an interest of mine. The avant-gardes were visionary because they opened new paths and ways of thinking. The early twentieth-century avant-gardes were already imagining the total artwork—and it's no coincidence that the project I curated after the '86 Biennale was called *Opera Totale*.

So this idea of exploring expressive languages that were more and more synesthetic, that involved all the senses, that opened up to new communicative forms—that captivated me from the moment I encountered *Crudelity Stoffe*.

With that openness, I began to dig deeper and write about these topics for *Zoom*. I also discovered other Italian groups that were active at the time, in the early 1980s—in Milan, in Naples. Along these research paths, I also came across what was then being called "communication art" or "telematic art". There was a group in Campania—with Giuseppe Salerno and other collaborators—that had begun serious reflections on these ideas.

Another key intuition I had was not to limit myself to what was happening in Italy. These groups, somehow, were already connected with half the world. So for me, it immediately became an international investigation.

Through this research into early computer art, I started to reconstruct the various points of connection. I also looked back at the history, focusing quite a bit on the 1960s—but that's another story. In my search for new developments and emerging groups, I came across Telematic Art.

So, in 1984—before the Biennale—I was offered a position thanks to the articles I had already written. It was for the *Festa Nazionale dell'Unità* in Pavia, specifically for the Cultural Heritage section, curated and directed by Giulio Carlo Argan. I organized an exhibition there, titled *Art and New Technologies*.

It included installations by Studio Azzurro, who had just begun working with the concept of nonlinear, fragmented narrative. I also presented various examples of computer art I had started collecting. And then there was this "telematic happening".

The telematic happening was a sort of art-lab based primarily on the fax machine—which had just become commercially available in the early 1980s. I brought together all these elements, and at that point, we began to organize ourselves and identify potential collaborators. That's when I discovered Roy Ascott in 1984, as well as Robert Adrian X in Australia, and our friends in Campania, around Giuseppe Salerno. Together we created, already in 1984, the first international network via fax, as part of the Pavia event.

At that time, I was focusing heavily on two things: on the one hand, computer graphics—which I recognized as an extraordinary field of inquiry—and on the other, telematic art and communication art. I began to dig into telematic and communication-based art, realizing that this was a history that had already begun in the 1970s. It was a fascinating lineage. I established contacts with as many people as I could reach, and I set up at least two or three significant labs.

One of them was a Telefax Art lab I organized in Turin, at the Castello del Valentino, with *Giovanotti Mondani Meccanici*, an avant-garde artistic group that had even appeared on television. They represented a very important part of Italy's underground scene at the time. They were working with computers, music, theatre, performance—a mix of hybrid and eclectic languages. I invited them to take part in a performance that was part of the programme I curated between Turin and Ivrea, titled *Macchinazione*.

Macchinazione was a moment curated together with an employee from RAI [Italian national broadcaster]. I was the curator and was given a 1-year appointment—rare and precious in those days—to develop a single, focused project. We created a multifaceted programme exploring how theatre had always approached technology, and how new technologies would ultimately reshape and rethink the theatrical experience. So this, too, happened before the Biennale in Venice.

With *Giovanotti Mondani Meccanici*, we staged this performance called *Telefax Art* at the Castello del Valentino. They performed it almost theatrically. The performance was recorded, scanned, and then faxed to our international partners—Australia, the UK, and more [Vienna, Pittsburgh, Melbourne, and Bristol]. The entire scenography of the performance was built using the material we received back, which had been reworked by these countries.

This is how my research really came to life—and it's still so alive that it led to the creation of MEET, with the idea of having a space that isn't just fixed and physical, but open and connected. That's what became MEET [Digital Culture Center in Milan].

Within this context, I became part of a network of researchers like Roy Ascott, Fred Forest, and Don Foresta, all of whom were working along similar lines.

How did I end up at the Venice Biennale? Roy called me and said, "Listen, we need to do a project at the Venice Biennale". But the Italian curator, Tommaso Trini, wasn't responding.

Here's some background you might already know: this pioneering exhibition—which we began working on in 1985—was organized using telecommunication methods. Don [Foresta], Roy [Ascott], Robert Adrian, Tommaso Trini, and I were all connected via Sharp, which had large servers in Toronto and a small satellite office in Milan. We were able to connect to the mainframe in Toronto, and they gave us access to send emails—which, back then, meant messages that were regularly printed out and physically downloaded. I still remember the punched paper printouts with all the correspondence.

The curators of a show about communication art and telematic art were actually working with telematic tools—though at the time we didn't even call it telematics, it was simply "informatics".

But then something happened: Tommaso Trini wasn't retrieving his messages. The server would get backed up, because that enormous server—well, maybe it had the memory capacity of my current cell phone—would freeze and stop functioning. The team in Toronto was desperate; they didn't know what to do. So Roy called me and asked me to help and to join the team.

For me, it was a pleasure to work with Tommaso Trini. He was brilliant. It was a joy to listen to him and to see how he interpreted this immaterial world—he really saw it clearly. So I supported him however I could. I would go to Sharp, which was in Milan, I think on Viale Abruzzi, and I'd download piles of material. That was our way of communicating—either you used the phone, which was extremely expensive, or you worked this way, which was much more coherent with the spirit of the project.

So the exhibition grew in tandem with our own experimentation in using these tools—it evolved from the very process we were engaged in. I found that absolutely fantastic. Roy invited me, I accepted, and together we began shaping the project we wanted to realize.

Right away, the idea emerged of creating a space that recalled the telematic "happenings" of the time—but also those from the 1970s, like *La Pissure du Texte*, *The Whole in the Space*, *The World in 24 Hours…* They were all laboratories. If you look at images of how these exchange, elaboration, co-creation, and participation events were conceived, you'd see that you were entering a lab-like space.

So at the Corderie [of the Arsenale at the Venice Biennale], the idea was to set up a lab environment, with a very 1980s spirit, where the potential of technology could be staged—but even more so, the communicative, artistic, and creative potential, especially in relation to telematic art.

At the Corderie, there was this section called *Planetary Network*, which I curated more directly, though there was more happening around it. There was a path that showed the evolution of 3D computer graphics curated by Valerio Eletti, projected nearby. There was a whole section dedicated to laserdiscs, because at the time, multimedia was beginning to be seen as a tool that could be used in museums. So there was this sense of staging visionary possibilities, even if they didn't quite develop in that direction—we had to wait until the 1990s and the CD. That was another part of the space.

So again, there was 3D graphics, tools for cultural heritage in the arts, tools for creating and processing art—and then this almost central zone, which was the *Planetary Network*. There, we involved a number of artists, including first and foremost Bruno Munari, with whom I had already collaborated on a similar happening in Pavia.

He was thrilled—after his experiments with Copy Art, he was here, you can also see his work, where he would send an image, it would come back, and we set up this "slow scan TV" system: on this screen, you could see a connection between two distant computers, and images would appear and form using this incredibly slow writing process.

There was a collective fax-based elaboration curated by—well, they didn't include the name, but it was Bruno Munari. One of the images he sent was returned to him; he was amazed, stretched it, and sent it back to Sydney. That day, I held a workshop with him. I also brought in another group, the Mida Group. Mida was composed of two twin brothers from Brescia [Gualtiero and Roberto Carraro], who were deeply interested in the subject. They had launched the idea of creating a new language, the *Mida Alphabet*. They began developing pictograms and synthesizing languages. "Ubiqua" was the name of my entire project, and they were the ones who managed that lab space on a daily basis. From time to time, we would have artists come in to experiment—especially with the fax.

FF: From an aesthetic point of view, did you have any particular sources of inspiration? What you're describing is a concept that doesn't really have a clear visual aesthetic. So how did you develop the aesthetic dimension of the project—if that was something you were interested in developing?

MGM: For me, the inspiration—and I'd say I was the one who gave the project this direction—came from the various centres focused on communication art. I had the intuition that with these tools—beyond simply creating an image or a video, even though computer art and 3D graphics were very active at the time—there was another layer. One of these tools was the fax, which I had just discovered. And going further back, there was slow-scan TV, and before that, the radio, and even satellite communication. Kit Galloway and Sherrie Rabinowitz, for instance, used satellites to connect New York with Los Angeles.

So I thought: *There's a future here. This is a world that is interconnected, collaborative, participatory, and co-creative.* There's a real-time dimension, a breakdown of physical and temporal boundaries. I grasped those concepts early on.

The aesthetic aspect that emerged was rooted in the idea of the lab: something contextualized in a specific space, but also open to other places. The vision came from the concepts that these artists and researchers were expressing in their work—breaking through space-time barriers, interactivity, co-creation, participation. All of it tied to a digital culture I was just beginning to explore. And even though the Web didn't exist yet—let's not forget that—we did have Internet in some form. We worked with Sharp, so connections were possible. These artists took tools meant for office or business use and repurposed them, bending their function towards creative and communicative ends.

To me, it felt like entering a vast laboratory imagining the future of a society that would communicate differently—very different from the mass communication we were used to, which was still predominantly TV or radio. Those were all broadcast models. But this broke the mould. It was highly experimental and pioneering: a fax machine, a mundane office tool for document transmission, became—thanks to these creative researchers—a device for interconnection, communication, and collective elaboration.

They pushed past the intended purpose of the technology. And I found that fantastic. That's exactly what the avant-garde does: it breaks out of existing frameworks and sees possibilities others don't. It projects an imaginative future, a society using these tools for collaboration, participation, and creative exchange.

That was their utopia. And so, aesthetically, what emerged was this pioneering, laboratory, creative spirit. That's what it was for me. Then, there were also the big screens. For me—and this has always been an obsession—those weren't just screens; they were walls being shattered, revealing something beyond. Real-time interaction came into the lab, exchanges happened live, and the space became performative as well.

So you had all of that. When the artists arrived, things would activate. That performative-laboratory aspect was central. That was the aesthetic of telematic art labs in the 1980s.

And of course, I didn't focus solely on that, even if my main contribution was the *Ubiqua* project. Around it, there was the whole broader context of digital experimentation at the time. We showcased tools that helped people understand where cultural heritage might be heading.

Remember, that Biennale edition was titled *Art, Science, and Technology*—so it was very much about bringing people into a space where art was in dialogue with science and tech, with scientific themes. That made it a very unique edition. But the people we called on to work on it were *artists*.

What I really wanted to do was to offer a vision of the digital dimension I was exploring—not just telematic art, even if that's what I focused on most. Thanks to these groups, I had the sense that something big was coming: a new kind of society that would communicate through entirely different means—far beyond TV, telephone, or radio. That was their strength.

FF: And within all this, was there a sense of hope about technology? Or was there also anxiety, unease?

MGM: Definitely hope—no unease. What has always fascinated me, whether I was working with computer art or anything else, was this powerful, disruptive message about the need to break cultural patterns and explore new expressive, linguistic, behavioural, and cognitive dimensions. That was their true scope.

In the movement of telematic art and communication, there was a strong emphasis on the democratization of tools. By connecting so many different places—Australia, for instance—it promised not a top-down broadcast model but a grassroots participatory exchange. That suggested an expansion of participatory and democratic models, and therefore, creative ones. And that fed into another dream of the time: the idea that we could finally have a creative lab available to everyone, using accessible tools.

The lab we set up at the Corderie was necessarily open by design—but even the labs these artists created, the happenings they organized, were open. The public took part. That generative power was incredibly strong, really powerful.

Then, when I later looked back at the 1960s, I saw this even more clearly. And when the Web finally arrived, I recognized it as the realization of what those early artists had anticipated. It became mainstream—what they had envisioned as early as the 1970s. The open Web truly did open the doors to the whole world, if you think about it.

At that point, their vision went mainstream—though, of course, other movements also emerged. But the same euphoria, the same energy, the same drive to explore and push boundaries—we felt all of that with the arrival of the Web. There was this magnificent, utopian dream that we'd finally have the tools and the lab, once again, where everyone could find their own space for expression and creation.

Then, sadly, that phase came to an end. A whole wave of economic development—the "Google economy", so to speak—somewhat disillusioned us. But still, that breakthrough, that urge to tear down hierarchical control of information, began with movements like this.

FF: So you spent the whole summer of 1986 in Venice?

MGM: Yes, absolutely. I was there the entire time. It was completely immersive. We had a whole schedule of events—other artists would come, discover the work, stay, and contribute. We built an actual program: connections with Sydney and elsewhere were scheduled and planned. It was maybe the most inspirational experience I've ever had, truly ahead of its time.

FF: What's your strongest memory of that summer and that project?

MGM: Oh… definitely the emotion of someone like Bruno Munari. He had already taken part in the event in Pavia, but this time he entered a kind of discovery mode—he didn't want to leave. He kept trying to generate images, asking others to manipulate and transform them. I was completely captivated. He had this quality that maybe belongs to the childlike stage of a person—or even of a society—this openness, this powerful desire to invent through experimentation. It was amazing to watch him work.

And I have to say, the public participation was also incredible. These were all new experiences. Sure, there had already been events in Italy—even beyond my own projects, there were things in places like Naples—but they remained niche experiments.

The strength of the Biennale was its ability to open up, to be truly disruptive, to legitimize and expose these practices to a broader public—one that wasn't at all specialized. And so there was wonder. You can't imagine the sense of wonder people felt when they saw an image leave and come back transformed, as if some kind of magic was unfolding before their eyes, almost in real time.

Wonder is a fundamental condition.

FF: And if there's a lesson you've carried with you from that experience to today?

MGM: Well, the fact is that no matter how much we build places of culture with walls and so on, walls don't really exist. Cultural processes should truly be in continuous osmosis. That really stayed with me—so much so that when I started launching initiatives, like Meet the Media Guru at the Mediateca here in Milan, I looked at the place and said: "Perfect. Here, the 'digital Templars' will gather, but I want to tear down the walls". And everyone said, "What are you talking about?"

Tearing down walls meant entering a diffuse communicative dimension that you could perceive in real time, not as a story someone documents and shows you later, but something you live and perceive in real time. So tearing down walls, to me, meant using projections, but above all, making sure that whoever is outside can come inside.

An event is localized, yes—but it belongs to the world the more you expand it, not just because I transmit it, but because I receive too. And I carried this input with me when I created Meet the Media Guru in 2005—so even years later—because that was my mindset.

And in 2005 it wasn't so common to create events with a webcam—I remember that spherical one—with minimal tools, where I would record, transmit, and receive, within something that looked like a conference but didn't want to be one, looked like a talk but didn't want to be a talk—it was called Meet the Media Guru, so this idea of encounter, exchange, real-time presence—and I took home with me the idea of events that were more exploratory, more dynamic, and that could be explored by breaking through physical dimensions.

And that's where all the thinking around real/virtual began. So that's what I took with me: the idea of a broader cultural dimension, a different space-time framework, but where interconnection is possible. And wherever it's possible, I still try to do that today.

FF: Are you still in touch with any of the original members of "Ubiqua" or the *Planetary Network*?

MGM: Well, I spoke with Roy Ascott some time ago, Robert unfortunately is no longer with us, and with Jévic—I don't even know if she's still around. But you know what? With the advent of the Web, when I saw how the world began tuning into this tool that literally broke down barriers, at that moment, I lost sight of that scene because art had become so strongly mainstream, and I dove into observing, more than anything, the social media landscape.

In Italy, I was perhaps one of the first to bring in the theme of virtual reality on the one hand—this theme of real space, virtual space, physical space, immaterial space, and so on. That was already present in the Venice lab too, but the other part was investigating more deeply the transformation of the world—especially communication—which was already being clearly questioned by those who had created the first social media as creative labs.

I saw this laboratory dimension of tools made available to break structures that were hierarchical or broadcast-based, however you want to call them. So I pursued more of that. No, I haven't had much contact except occasionally with Roy—we still touch base now and then. In fact, I even went when he was awarded the big prize in Linz, when he received recognition as a pioneer.

Right now, I couldn't say what kind of reflection he's focusing on because all this historical aspect is grand. We should take all those literary pages and read them, looking at what has actually changed through the most powerful art-communication or telematic tool, which is the Internet combined with the Web, because that's where everything really took off.

FF: Listening to you talk about your memories from '86 until today, it seems like you followed a completely linear path—as if the way was already paved. How did you experience that path? How did you see it while you were walking it?

MGM: Instinctively, I always stuck to a red thread: looking at the world of art, looking at those I considered artists. Defining who an artist is is difficult for me, but instinctively, in the field of new media, that was the area I was interested in. I studied photography and the early twentieth-century avant-gardes that worked with cinema—that was my focus. And I must say, they had such a disruptive power through which social change could be glimpsed. For me, it has always been a bit like that.

So, when I encountered "Crudelity Stoffe", I looked backward and forward, trying to keep a steady course. Through the most creative, visionary, and imaginative research, I tried to understand how much they really anticipated. That was my game. I trained myself to understand what could seriously become developments beyond individual projects.

In that way, I built myself a kind of compass, with a needle that could recognize the cardinal points. I had the time to train myself—as I always say—because not many people were working on this at the time, although there was always a good audience when you held an event. I had the time to observe, study, reflect, undisturbed. I'd do maybe one or two events a year and almost appropriate the energy coming from all this research, which helped me broaden my perspective. I brought all these elements together.

So I played a bit the role of an interpreting curator, trying to tell these stories. In my way, perhaps even a bit artistically. Thanks to these encounters, I traced, intercepted, and identified paths belonging to art that I recognized, but I also discovered new directions that all proved timely, so I'm very satisfied.

I never got scattered; I explored many directions, but they didn't belong to different stories—it was a single scene. For me, it was a continuous exploration.

FF: What's the most creative part of your work from that period that you've carried with you until today?

MGM: Trying to intuit where the core of the matter lay—not just the fascination with technology for its own sake. It was this creative thought that I saw taking shape, announcing something that would change. That was wonderful.

Another point was the desire—and maybe this is my nature, also as a former middle school teacher—to communicate it back. So if I understood this thing and it was true, and I had demonstrations, how do I bring these pieces of information together and how do I tell the story?

And how I told it could be an exhibition, a conference, a series—something that let this urgent subject become common heritage. I didn't keep it to myself, I don't know how to say it. So I really enjoyed organizing my thinking in space.

FF: Did you ever feel frustrated by a technology that wasn't yet available? Or did you have a contrary attitude in the sense of…

MGM: No. In my work, I never felt the urgency to tinker with technology, because with the famous early 1980s, I grasped what was important for me to make clear: that this technological world that was taking shape already contained important cultural aspects. That's what interested me. So understanding these processes or intuiting what changes they would bring was my research, my way of doing research. I never felt frustrated by technology.

In some way, I made myself a sort of small guide because I could see the evolution, and time helped me there. I went to SIGGRAPH every year and saw creative processes with 3D images advance and peek into market sectors like cinema.

Many people were very reluctant—for example, in cinema, I spoke with Carlo Rambaldi, Gillo Pontecorvo, Maselli—all people who, except Gillo who was curious, lacked curiosity. They saw special effects as a threat and didn't see the film industry was changing. But I saw the film industry was changing, and I said, "the whole process will be digital". And I was right.

FF: Is there something you haven't done yet that you would like to accomplish?

MGM: Yes, well, the first thing — that pile of stuff you see there — is a book that's been stalled since 2004. It's called *The New Visible*. It has a title, some chapters, but it's been stuck. Aside from the book, which maybe I should do sooner or later (though I'd have to stop doing operational work), what I really want to do is a big exhibition about the Italian scene I lived through, especially the 1980s. It would help me recover parts that I've somehow absorbed and internalized, but maybe never really reflected on deeply.

It's like my brain was producing independently from me. I'd love to find the time and space to pick up, organize, and rediscover the meaning of everything I did better, and I want to make a big show about it.

For this exhibition I have in mind, MEET alone is not enough, because it's a scene I want to tell in an international context and linked to art. Because what happened is not disconnected, from an expressive or creative point of view, from some artistic movements. It's very much connected to expectations, research, trends, and movements in art history.

I feel the need to put the Italian scene in order, because I lived it. I also experienced it somewhat by reconnecting with some Italian pioneers from the 1960s. So it would be interesting to tell that story—not so much as essayistic research, but as a lived history.

And I want the international scene, especially that decade—the 1980s and 1990s until the advent of the Web—with a whole chapter on programmed art and a historical theme that I want to revisit. So yes, that's an exhibition I really want to do. I want to really revive that spirit of deep research.

FF: I understand. At least from what I've studied and tried to understand by reading and looking at those catalogues, it was a lively, experimental period, without restraints, maybe unlike now…

MGM: You said it well—without restraints. The artists themselves truly felt like avant-gardes. I call them pioneers, because I saw this impact on society at all levels, and a connection to history. I understood that. And like them, I had no restraints either, because I always did whatever I wanted. There was curiosity, and since no one was really under the spell of one hype or another, I could sow the directions I discovered.

Yes, it's true, that was a very experimental and open period in that sense. Then, of course, came all the complaints afterward—because it was a cultural and artistic form not well supported or recognized. The media, up to 2000, never really woke up to this stuff, so there wasn't much real media backing. But that complaint is also somewhat futile, because if I think of all the initiatives I've done—and there are many—I've always done them with public and cultural institutions. So there was some attention, it's not like there was none, including the Biennale.

FF: And in that sense, how did you relate to the completely conservative institutions?

MGM: I was lucky, or maybe it wasn't luck. Since there is always someone curious about the new, in the case of the Venice Film Festival it was Gillo Pontecorvo; in the case of the 1986 Venice Biennale's *Art, Science and Technology* exhibition, it was Roy Ascott—invited by Maurizio Calvesi—and Carlo Giulio Argan in Pavia. So it's not true that there were no attentive intellectuals.

It just didn't become a mainstream topic, or the theme of new art or culture with a capital C. So it was a metaphorical laboratory, a truly great lab for everyone.

FF: It's nice to hear your memories because when I wrote my doctoral thesis on the history of how technologies entered the Venice Biennale from the 1960s on, and when I read about the 1970s and the first serious computer art show at the Biennale, the critical attitude was not so much one of amazement but rather fear and putting up defences. But then seeing how things developed with you in the 1980s is as if the Biennale had…

MGM: Not just the Biennale of the 1980s, but also the 1990s, with Fausto Colombo—we did retrospectives on computers in cinema and cinema in computers, computer graphics shows, etc. Then there was that 2-year appointment with Gillo Pontecorvo. These were always very open spaces. Again, sure, there was an audience, but there were also curators. People always make the difference, clearly, as always.

FF: Do you think that cinema has somewhat helped to convey these messages better than visual art or architecture?

MGM: Cinema definitely opened more breaches in this direction, but for example regarding all the research that later developed around the Web, cinema had little to do with it. The art world has always been resistant. The art world and the art ecosystem continued to be resistant, just as it was for many years with photography and video art. Eventually, they accept it, but they have to find their economic formula—because if they don't find that, they won't move. So except for a few courageous curators who carefully craft their programming including art that uses these languages, you don't find much space in the art ecosystem.

It's more a development welcomed in cinema, special effects, games, and the other development is in communication—new narrative video forms, new immersive audience engagement—but these do not belong to the art ecosystem.

One has to gradually try to better connect these aspects, insisting that we are still talking about art—although not everyone who uses digital technologies feels like an artist. That's not really the case, as we know. There is still a lot of work to do.

I have to say it's easier in other countries for this discourse to be accepted—for example, the Whitney, MoMA—because their cultural background is new. They don't have the heavy burden that we have here in Italy with our cultural heritage—long live that heritage—but with all institutions focused on conserving that heritage.

There, abroad, energies can be freed in other directions. Think about the work MoMA and Whitney have done, and all the new museums abroad—they have a different vibrancy and dynamism.

Meanwhile, the work is a bit heavier in Europe, particularly in Italy, I'd say. France is a bit ahead, but if you listen to them, they all complain too. However, they have serious funding in this sector; we do not.

If you move away from cinema, there are no funding sources going in this direction.

FF: Thanks so much, Maria Grazia. It's been really inspiring to chat with you and revisit such ground-breaking work—from *Planetary Network* to *Ubiqua*. What you've shared not only highlights the incredible innovation at the heart of those projects but also sheds light on how much the cultural context shapes what's possible. The challenges you mention in Italy really resonate, and make your achievements all the more remarkable. I'm excited to see how MEET continues to carry that energy forward.

Biographical Note

Maria Grazia Mattei is a journalist and art critic who has been exploring the social, cultural, and anthropological dimensions of digital culture since 1982. Born in Pisa, she holds a degree in Art Criticism from the Istituto di Storia dell'Arte in Milan. In 1995 she founded Mattei Digital Communication, a research and communication centre dedicated to the study, dissemination, and promotion of new media culture. Since 2005, she has directed Meet the Media Guru, an international program of talks and debates with leading figures in digital culture, widely recognized as a key platform for critical reflection on digital innovation. In 2018, with the support of Fondazione Cariplo, she founded MEET – the International Centre for Digital Culture in Milan. Mattei has organized and curated numerous initiatives in collaboration with major institutions including the Venice Biennale, Digifest (Toronto), SIGGRAPH (USA), and Imagina (France). She curated *Pixar. 25 Years of Animation* (2011) and the Italian edition of *Pixar. 30 Years of Animation* (2018). She has served on the Central Grant Committee of Fondazione Cariplo (2013–2019) and sits on the Board of Directors of Artemide.

Conclusions

The exploration of computational art within the context of the Venice Biennale is not merely a recounting of events but a journey through the evolution of ideas, technologies, and artistic expressions. Each chapter in this edited book serves as a portal into the unique experiences and creative processes of artists who have left an indelible mark on the intersection of art and technology.

The contributions of Simon Pope, Tamiko Thiel, Joseph Nechvatal, Fré Ilgen, Maureen Kendal, Frieder Nake, Paul Thomas, Maria Grazia Mattei, and Francesca Franco within the historical and political narrative of the Venice Biennale offer a fascinating intersection of tradition, rebellion, and recognition.

Historically, the Venice Biennale has its roots deeply entrenched in the celebration of academic styles, representing a conservative stance towards art. However, the political and social upheavals of 1968 brought about a transformative "anomaly" in the Biennale's curatorial model. The introduction of new technologies, coupled with the political fervour of the time, allowed the institution to break away from its traditional Salon model. This marked a pivotal moment in the acceptance of media art, eventually leading to the landmark 1970 exhibition, *Research and Planning—Proposals for an Experimental Exhibition*, curated by Umbro Apollonio and Dietrich Mahlow.

Simon Pope's chapter, reflecting on his representation of Wales in the 2003 Biennale, unfolds as a narrative of transformation. Beyond the physical space of the Biennale, it navigates the evolving landscape of his artistic concepts, revealing the living entity of his work, shaped continuously by time and experience. This narrative becomes a part of the larger historical and political context, showcasing not only the evolution of Pope's work but also the Biennale's gradual openness to new forms of artistic expression. It signifies an ongoing shift from a conservative stance to a more inclusive and experimental approach, illustrating the dynamic relationship between artists and the changing ethos of the Venice Biennale over time.

Tamiko Thiel's exploration of Manifest.AR's augmented reality intervention in 2011 is a testament to the Biennale's responsiveness to technological advancements.

F. Franco (ed.), *Computational Art at the Venice Biennale (1970–2015)*, Springer Series on Cultural Computing, https://doi.org/10.1007/978-3-032-04258-3

The chapter delves into the intricacies of geolocative augmented reality, demonstrating how technology can be a medium for global collaboration, transcending physical boundaries and redefining the viewer's relationship with art in a specific context. The global collaboration showcased in her chapter mirrors the shifting landscape of artistic collaboration and interaction, echoing the broader societal changes that influenced the Biennale's trajectory.

Joseph Nechvatal's chapter adds another layer to the historical context. Nechvatal introduces the concept of "vOluptuary drOid décOlletage" within the framework of the 55th International Art Exhibition in 2013. This chapter not only illustrates Nechvatal's work but also delves into the philosophical underpinnings of *Noise*, revealing how the artist conceptualizes and communicates the "art of noise" within the immersive setting of the Biennale. His work within the collateral event *Noise* aligns with the exploration of unconventional forms of artistic expression, challenging the status quo. Nechvatal's inclusion highlights the evolution of the Biennale, embracing new ideas and pushing artistic boundaries.

Fré Ilgen's experience in the collateral event *Frontiers Reimagined* during the 2015 Biennale becomes a reflection of the institution's willingness to engage with diverse perspectives. The interaction between the artist and the unique environment of Palazzo Grimani becomes a story of symbiosis, where the historical backdrop of Venice converges with contemporary artistic expressions, creating a dialogue between tradition and innovation.

Maureen Kendal's review of Orly Aviv's *Nervous Organ* and the author's interview with Frieder Nake add critical dimensions to the narrative. Kendal's contribution provides a lens through which the audience can re-examine the digital interactive installation showcased at the 2015 Biennale, emphasizing the importance of critical discourse in understanding and appreciating the nuances of computational art.

Frieder Nake's interview introduces a historical dimension, harking back to the roots of computer art with Nake's participation in the first computer art show at the Biennale in 1970. While capturing the essence of Nake's art, this interview serves as a bridge connecting the early pioneers of computer art with the contemporary explorations showcased in the book.

Paul Thomas's wide-ranging interview provides a vital perspective on the evolving landscape of media art through the lens of the 1986 Venice Biennale. His reflections on artistic integrity, institutional frameworks, and the challenges of digital preservation enrich the dialogue on how artists negotiate the tensions between creativity and institutional constraints. Thomas's call for more organic, artist-led approaches to archiving and discourse adds an essential critical voice to this collection.

Maria Grazia Mattei's interview offers a compelling account of Italy's engagement with digital culture from the 1980s onward. As a journalist, critic, and founder of MEET, she traces the trajectory of new media art and its social implications, highlighting early telematic art's utopian spirit and its legacy. Her reflections underscore the crucial role of public engagement and institutional support in nurturing experimental digital practices within a traditionally conservative art context.

The author's article concludes the selection of contributions by exploring the impact of new media art on the Venice Biennale's original curatorial model, examining how technology brought both a wave of creativity and a destabilizing element to the traditional structure of the institution post-1968.

Together, these discussions contribute to the ongoing dialogue about the acceptance and evolution of computer art within the Biennale. In the larger historical and political context, this book's exploration of computational art serves as a microcosm of the Biennale's journey. From its initial conservative stance to the radical shifts of 1968, the gradual embrace of technology in the 1980s, and the eventual acceptance of art and technology in the 1990s, the contributions here become chapters in the larger story of the Venice Biennale's evolution. They showcase not only the artists' individual narratives but also the symbiotic relationship between the Biennale and the changing tides of artistic and technological innovation over time.

www.ingramcontent.com/pod-product-compliance
Lightning Source LLC
Chambersburg PA
CBHW070330060426
42428CB00071B/2533
9783032042576